Alfred Kirchhoff

**Volapük**

Or, universal language. A short grammatical course

Alfred Kirchhoff

**Volapük**
*Or, universal language. A short grammatical course*

ISBN/EAN: 9783337084400

Printed in Europe, USA, Canada, Australia, Japan

Cover: Foto ©Paul-Georg Meister /pixelio.de

More available books at **www.hansebooks.com**

# VOLAPÜK

OR

# UNIVERSAL LANGUAGE.

*A SHORT GRAMMATICAL COURSE.*

BY

ALFRED KIRCHHOFF,

*Professor of Geography at the University of Halle.*

*AUTHORIZED TRANSLATION.*

THIRD EDITION, IMPROVED, AMENDED, AND ENLARGED.
WITH A NEW
VOLAPÜK-ENGLISH AND ENGLISH-VOLAPÜK VOCABULARY

LONDON:
SWAN SONNENSCHEIN & CO.,
PATERNOSTER SQUARE.
1888.

# PREFACE.

Of the existence of this new language, Volapük, some reports have from time to time crossed our Channel, and newspaper paragraphs have treated it with good-natured banter, which, however, did not benefit the movement.

It must be confessed that, in one respect, Volapük is no exception to all the other languages; it sounds comic and outlandish to him that is ignorant of it. Anent this, it is worth while to quote an old Shakespearian joke:—

KATH: "*Comment appelez-vous le pied et la robe?*"

. . . . . . . .

KATH: " . . . . *O Seigneur Dieu! ce sont des mots de son mauvais, corruptible, gros et impudique, et non pour les dames d'honneur d'user; je ne voudrais prononcer ces mots devant les seigneurs de France pour tout le monde.*"

Such is the opinion entertained by fair Katharine of English, the most beautiful and most vigorous of all languages. But she did not know that she was prejudiced, and that banter and ridicule are not argument.

The questions we have to deal with are:—

1. Is a Universal Language desirable and attainable? And,—

2. If so, does "Volapük," the invention of Johann Martin Schleyer (now of Constance), possess the qualifications needful for a Universal Language?

The want of a Universal Means of Communication has often been felt and expressed by both scholars and merchants; the former have long been conscious of the inadequacy of Latin to satisfy modern requirements, and the latter have not even this means at their disposal; and yet year by year does this want make itself more strongly felt, as the means of communication by steam and electricity multiply and extend. Hence the necessity of spending much time and labour in the acquisition of languages; how economical then, in the best sense of the word, would it prove, if all this effort could be saved!

In fact, language is not the only sphere of human activity where Universality has been sought, sometimes with and sometimes without success. Among the failures may be counted the ambitious search after the Philosopher's Stone, the Doctor's Panacea or Universal Medicine, and the Chemist's Universal Solvent; but there are also some successes to be recorded. The Metric System is on the high road to become the Universal System of Weights and Measures, and Decimal Fractions owe their great popularity to their being the nearest approach to a Universal Denominator to all fractions. Why should language be judged *a priori* to fall inevitably into the category of failures? Englishmen, with their world-wide empire and interests, should be the first to heartily welcome the attempt to supply a World-Speech.

Now this is just what Volapük does, and in the easiest possible manner into the bargain. The vocabulary consists mostly of simplified English and German words (rarely of Latin or French terms), and the Grammar is so simple that it can be learnt in a few days. This gratifying result is due to the language being freed from all exceptions, irregularities, idioms, and useless complexities of arbitrary genders, of declensions and conjugations, the bequests of centuries and chiliads of use, wear and tear, and individual caprice—of fossil remains and linguistic records of prehistoric events. It requires already a considerable knowledge of the language to be able to look for *tetigisti* under *tango*, for *hieb* under *hauen*, and for *je puis* under *pouvoir*. In fact, in all languages, except Volapük, the dictionary is of most use to him that could very nearly do without it. But when the Volapükist has once mastered his short grammar, he at once steps, with the help of the dictionary, into the full use of the language. The difficulties of construing, spelling, and pronunciation resemble in Volapük the famous snakes of Iceland; they have no existence.

In composition, the order of words is nearly identical with the translucent arrangement of an English phrase.

Some suggest, not without good show of reason, that English should be adopted as the Universal Language; but, much as might justly be urged in favour of this proposal, there is this one consideration fatal to its speedy adoption: English is difficult to acquire. *Experto crede.* It presents itself to the foreigner as a long series of idioms and synonyms, as singular and insular in their character as Englishmen themselves are. On the very threshold of the language he encounters the perplexities of its peculiar spelling. No doubt all this is surmountable, and if, or when, by the process of Natural Selection English shall in due time have superseded all other languages, then Volapük will disappear as useless; but it will meanwhile have rendered very great service.

As for the work here submitted to the English reader, it is a translation of the excellent grammar of Professor Alfred Kirchhoff, of Halle, which has passed through three large editions in less than six months, and I can do no better than translate a few passages from the three German prefaces.

## FROM THE PREFACE TO THE FIRST GERMAN EDITION.

"Volapük is beyond doubt destined to become the language of communication among all nations. Every nation will continue to speak its own language; but those who follow pursuits, be they merchants or scholars, where international communication is indispensable, should study this world-speech, so as to save themselves the endless toil and regrettable loss of time consequent on the study of at least twelve European languages."

" The study of Volapük is spreading over all the cultured states of Europe, and into the civilized countries beyond the ocean. Thus then Volapük is not a still-born child."

## FROM THE PREFACE TO THE SECOND GERMAN EDITION.

" Any one who has acquired in a few days the elements of this World-Speech, so far as to be able to write with the help of the Dictionary a letter in Volapük, can at once enter into correspondence with all the civilized nations of the globe, without the necessity of studying their several languages. Prof. Kerckhoffs, of Paris, in his excellent periodical *Le Volapük, revue mensuelle*, keeps a register with addresses of all Volapükists in and beyond Europe, who are able and willing to conduct correspondence with Volapükists of other nations. . . . On the circulars of large commercial firms we not uncommonly meet with the phrase '*Spodon Volapüko*'—'Correspondence conducted in Volapük,' so that a German merchant, for example, can communicate with his Portuguese, Spanish, Russian, or

Chinese business friends with as much ease as now he can correspond with Frenchmen or Englishmen, with whose languages he is familiar."

## FROM THE PREFACE TO THE THIRD GERMAN EDITION.

"Although the second edition was of double the size of the first, it yet did not suffice to supply the ever growing demand for this grammar for more than a few months, so persistent and expanding is the study of this World-Speech."

"This new edition has supplied the opportunity to utilize the highly valuable suggestions made to the Author by Prof. Kerckhoffs of Paris. Every expression or phrase that had a specifically German flavour about it, and was thus wholly unsuited to the classic simplicity of a World-Speech, has been eliminated, and moot points were settled."

"Prof. Kerckhoffs' admirable '*Cours complet de Volapük*' will shortly appear in German garb, as a more advanced course to this present work."

P.S.—Whilst these pages were going through the press, a fourth and a fifth edition already appeared, such are the strides that Volapük is making in Germany. This translation has had the benefit of profiting by all the successive improvements, and my warmest thanks are due to Prof. A. Kirchhoff, of the University of Halle, for the cordial sympathy he has evinced for this work, and for the persistent and self-denying help he has afforded me.

A. S.

## PREFACE TO THE SECOND ENGLISH EDITION.

Hardly more than a week has elapsed since the first publication of this work, when already a second edition is called for,—a proof as convincing as it is gratifying of the interest the public is taking in this movement.

The reprint has afforded the opportunity of making a few corrections necessitated by the improvements and alterations made in the language since the first edition went though the press.

A small chapter has been added on Euphony and Word-building A. S.

# PREFACE TO THE THIRD ENGLISH EDITION.

This new edition has been amended and enlarged in several essential particulars. The translator's cordial thanks are due to the eminent and learned Volapükist, Professor A. Kerckhoffs, of Paris, at whose suggestion several defects and deficiencies, hardly avoidable in the earlier editions, have been remedied.

A few words of explanation seem desirable. In the growth of this new language two tendencies have manifested themselves: the one aims at such amplification and minute precision as will make Volapük co-extensive with German; the other strives for conciseness and classic simplicity in the vocabulary and in the grammar and for emancipation from the German type. In fact, Volapük, an artificial language though it be, is still subject to laws of its own, and the endeavour to form it after a certain extraneous model must be regarded as an error. This present Grammar rejects all redundancy and superfluity, and thus sides with the emancipating school.

On one point it is advisable to forewarn the reader. A mere literal word-for-word translation into Volapük is not likely to yield a result that is easily intelligible. A good translator must be able to distinguish between the literal and the figurative sense of words, as only the former expressions admit of a strictly verbal transfer. But this distinction is not easy to him who has a scanty knowledge of his own mother-tongue. Although Volapuk can be learnt without an acquaintance with a foreign tongue, yet he that knows another language besides his own will, even in the use of Volapük, have the advantage over him that lacks the aid afforded by comparing his own language with at least one foreign speech.

A. S.

# INDEX.

|   | PAGE |
|---|---|
| Accent | 9 |
| Articles | 9 |
|     Accusative and Dative, position of | 12 |
| Adjectives, Comparison of | 15 |
|     In *ik* or *lik* | 14 |
|     Position of | 14 |
|     Used substantively | 14 |
| Adverbs, comparison of | 15 |
| Euphony, Rules of | 53 |
| Feminine Prefix | 14 |
| Groups of Words | 13 |
| Infinitival Ending | 12 |
| *Ji*, Feminine Prefix | 14 |
| Negation | 12 |
| Nouns, Compound | 15 |
|     Declension of | 9 |
|     Gender of | 12 |
|     Proper, Declension of | 36 |
| Names of Days of the Week | 34 |
|     Of the Months | 34 |
|     Seasons | 34 |
|     Sciences | 35 |
| Numerals | 16, 19, 21, 23 |
|     Cardinals rendered Ordinals | 26 |
|     Distributive | 29 |
|     Multiplicative | 29 |
|     Ordinals used adverbially | 26 |
|     Repetitive | 27 |
| Participles | 31 |
| Person, second, use of | 12 |
| Plural of Nouns, Formation of | 10 |
| Prefixes,— | |
|     *da*; *fe* and *fö* | 36 |
|     *di*; *ge* | 40 |
|     *ji* | 14 |
|     *le*; *sma* | 18 |
|     *li*; *lu* | 17 |
|     *ne* | 23 |

|  | PAGE |
|---|---|
| Prepositions followed by Nominative | 10 |
| Pronouns, Indefinite *os* | 12, 14 |
|     Personal | 14 |
|     Possessive | 14 |
|     Demonstrative | 14 |
|     Reciprocal and Reflective | 32 |
|     Relative | 14 |
| Pronunciation | 9 |
| Question—particle *li* | 17 |
| Suffixes,— | |
|     *ad; ef* | 36 |
|     *än; op; öp; üd* | 39 |
|     *äl; am; av; ed* | 35 |
|     *el* | 13, 26 |
|     *af; em; en; ö; öf; öm; ü; ug; üp* | 40 |
|     *id; o; öd; ös* | 26 |
|     *ik; lik* | 14 |
|     *il* | 17 |
|     *la* | 28 |
|     *na* | 27 |
|     *nik; öv* | 29 |
|     *öl* | 31 |
|     *ul* | 34 |
|     *um; ün* | 15 |
| Tense-prefixes applied to Nouns | 20 |
| Verbs, Conditional | 29 |
|     Conjugation of | 11 |
|     Imperative | 26 |
|     Infinitive | 12 |
|     Passive Voice | 22 |
|     Reciprocal and Reflective | 32 |
|     Subjunctive | 28 |
|     Tenses, Formation of | 20 |
| Vocabulary | 56 |
| Words, Groups of | 13, 52 seq. |

# VOLAPÜK OR UNIVERSAL LANGUAGE.

## § I. ON PRONUNCIATION AND ACCENT.

(*a*) The vowels *a, e, i, o, u* are pronounced as in the following English words :—

a as in *father, rather*   o as in *go, no*
e as *a* in *pate, mane*   u „   „ *glue, rue*
i as *i* in *give, live*

Modified vowels, *ä, ö, ü*, are sounded as in the German *Väter, Götter*, and *Mütter*.

Two vowels together are pronounced separately, and never united into a diphthong; thus *au* reads a-u, *ea* reads e-a (like ay-ah), and so on.

(*b*) The consonants have the same functions as in English, with the exception of—
  *g*, which is always hard.
  *c*,   „   „ sounded like the "ch" in our *chill*.
  *j*,   „   „   „   „   „ "sh"   „   „ *shot*.
  *y* is also sounded as in English in *yet;* and
  *z* like *ts*.

(*c*) The last syllable of the word is always accented. Thus we say măn, not măn, mānâ (mānāh).

(*d*) Proper names retain their peculiar spelling and pronunciation.

The letter *q* does not occur in Volapük, but it is used in proper names to express the guttural sound of the German *ch* in *ich*, and of the Spanish *j* in *Apuljaras*. Thus *München* (Munich) is *Münqen*, and *Apuljaras* is *Apulqaras*. The accent in proper names is indicated by the circumflex (ˆ) in long, and by grave (`) in short vowels; thus *Perû* and *Mèqiko*.

## § II. GRAMMAR.

### § 1.

ARTICLES are not used in Volapük.

### § 2.

DECLENSION OF NOUNS.

| SINGULAR. | PLURAL. |
|---|---|
| N. *fat*, father | *fats*, fathers |
| G. *fata*, of the father | *fatas*, of the fathers |
| D. *fate*, to the father | *fates*, to the fathers |
| A. *fati*, father | *fatis*, fathers |

One inspection shows that the genitive is formed by suffixing *a*; dative, *e*; accusative, *i*; and that the plural takes in all cases an additional *s*. The vocative can be indicated by the interjection *o*.

§ 3

Prepositions are followed by the nominative. "In" is translated by *in*, and "into" by *al*; thus: in the garden, at school, *in gad, in jul*; into the garden, *al gad*.

VOCABULARY I.

*badik*, bad
*binom*, (he) is
*binoms*, (they) are
*buk*, book
*cil*, child
*dog*, dog
*dom*, house
*domo*, at home
*e*, and
*fat*, father
*gad*, garden
*gadel*, gardener
*gletik*, large, big, great, [long
*goloms*, (they) go
*gudik*, good, well

*i*, also
*jul*, school
*julel*, scholar, pupil
*ko*, with
*labom*, (he) has
*laboms*, (they) have
*lob*, praise
*lobom*, (he) praises
*loboms*, (they) praise
*lönom*, (he) belongs
*man*, man
*mot*, mother
*neif*,* knife
*son*, son
*u*, or

EXERCISE 1.

(a) Translate into English:
1. Binom badik.
2. Fat binom gudik.
3. Fat e mot binoms gudik.
4. Cil labom buki.
5. Neif lönom gadele.
6. Dog mana binom gletik.
7. Julel labom bukis e neifis.
8. Loboms sonis mana.
9. Dom lönom mote cilas.
10. Fat binom domo e i mot.
11. Julels goloms al jul u ko fat al gad.
12. O fat, neifs lönoms sones gadela.

---

* Read ne-if, see § 1, (a).

(b) Translate into Volapük.
1. The praise of the father is great.
2. The books of the pupils are good.
3. He praises the house of the gardener.
4. The knife belongs to the father and to the mother; it also belongs to the sons.
5. O mother, men are bad.
6. They have knives and also books.
7. The father of the gardener has the dog of the mother.
8. The pupils are in the garden, and have the dogs of the man.
9. The sons of the gardener are at home, or in the garden of the father.
10. The children go with the father and the mother into the garden.
11. Father and mother praise the children of the gardener.
12. The pupils have the books in the school.

## § 4.
### Conjugation of Verbs.

Verbs are conjugated by suffixing the personal pronoun to the stem of the verb; thus: *Lobom*, he praises, is literally "praises he," *om* meaning "he."

From the stem of the verb "to have," which in Volapük is *lab* (not *hab*)* we form:

*labob*, I have (*ob*, I)  *labobs*, we have (*obs*, we)
*labol*, thou hast (*ol*, thou)  *labols*, ye have (*ols*, ye)
*labom*, he has (*om*, he)  *laboms*, they have (*oms*, they, masc.)  [fem.]
*labof*, she has (*of*, she)  *labofs*, they have (*ofs*, they,
*labon*,†one has (*on*, French;
 *on*, German *man*)
*labos*, it has (*os*, it)

---

\* In Volapük an initial *h* is frequently changed into *l*, to suit the taste of many nations who have a dislike to an initial *h*.
† Contrast:
  *ob*, I, with *obs*, we.    *om*, he, with *oms*, they (masc.).
  *ol*, thou, with *ols*, ye.   *of*, she, with *ofs*, they (fem.).

In Volapük every noun is masculine, except those signifying a female, which are of feminine gender, and therefore the terminations *of* and *ofs* are used only with females; thus: *mot labof*, the mother has; and *mots labofs*, the mothers have. With all other nouns the verb terminates in *om*; thus: *jul binom gletik*, the school is large; *neifs binoms gudik*, the knives are good.

The termination *os* is only used indefinitely; thus: *binos gudik*, it is good.

For the second person singular, the Volapükist, like the Quaker, uses "thou" in all cases.

The Infinitival ending is *ön*, e.g., *labön*, to have.

The negative *no* is placed before the verb; thus: "he has not" is *no labom*.

The Accusative (*régime direct*) precedes the Dative (*régime indirect*); thus: "he gives the child wine," is translated into Volapük by, "he gives wine (to) the child."

### VOCABULARY II.

*ab*, but
*das*, that (conjn.)
*denu*, again
*dlefön*, to hit
*dut*, industry
*dutik*, industrious
*jutön*, to shoot
*kuk*, kitchen
*kukel*, cook
*kukön*, to cook
*liev* (li-ev), hare
*lilön*, to hear
*lobön*, to praise
*löfön*, to love
*logön*, to see

*men*, human being (Lat. homo)
*saun* (sa-un), health
*saunik*, healthy, in good health, wholesome
*stäg*, stag
*sup*, soup
*tid*, act of teaching, lesson
*tidel*, teacher
*tidön*, to teach
*töt*, thunder
*ya*, already
*yag*, the chase, the hunt
*yagön*, to hunt
*yagel*, huntsman

### EXERCISE 2.

(*a*) Translate into English:
1. No löfobs yagi.
2. Yagel jutom stägis e lievis.
3. Mot kukof cile denu supi.

4. Yagels laboms dogis.
5. Jutob, ab no dlefob.
6. Logon domis e manis.
7. Lilol töti.
8. Binos gudik, das cils binoms dutik.
9. Lilob, das no binol saunik.
10. Lobols sauni menas.
11. Tidel tidom cilis.
12. Lobon duti julelas.

(b) Translate into Volapük.
1. The men hunt the stag.
2. The mother is well again; she is in the kitchen.
3. The mothers love the children.
4. Thou shootest, but thou dost not hit the hare (say "thou hittest not").
5. It is good that we do not hear the thunder.
6. Ye hear the lesson.
7. The son is well again, but he does not go to school. (Say, "he goes not to school.")
8. The cook's soup is bad.
9. Men love dogs.
10. They (fem.) are good.
11. O pupils, you are not industrious.
12. You (2nd pers. pl.) see the house of the father.

§ 5. OF GROUPS OF WORDS.

The noun indicating the fundamental notion is mostly a monosyllable consisting of two consonants and a vowel between them, as *tid* and *yag*. The infinitive of the corresponding verb is formed by adding the termination *ön*; and the agent performing the action is indicated by the suffix *el\**; thus:

*tid*, teaching, les- *yag*, the chase, *kuk*, kitchen
    son              the hunt     *kukön*, to cook
*tidön*, to teach  *yagön*, to hunt  *kukel*, (a) cook
*tidel*, the teacher *yagel*, the huntsman

---

\* This termination has the same function as the English suffix *er* in "brew*er*," "teach*er*," etc. In Volapük *l* is frequently put in the place of *r* (thus "beer" is *bil*), for the sake of nations like the Chinese, who either do not possess the *r* or find it difficult to pronounce it accurately.

The feminine sex is indicated by prefixing *ji-** to the corresponding masc. noun; thus:

{ *son*, son       { *tidel*, teacher, master
{ *jison*, daughter { *jitidel*, female teacher, mistress

Adjectives end in *ik* or *lik*, thus:

*gud*, good-  *saun*, health     *yun*, youth (abstr. noun,
ness         *saunik*, healthy   Lat. *juventa*)
*gudik*, good                    *yunik*, young ·
                                 *yunlik*, youthful

## § 6.

Adjectives are used substantively by the addition of *el*, e.g. *gudikel*, the good (man); *jigudikel*, the good woman.

The adjective follows the substantive (in harmony with the common usage of placing the secondary after the primary), and is undeclined; e.g. *fat gudik*, the good father; *julel dutik*, the industrious pupil.

## § 7.

PERSONAL PRONOUNS are declined like nouns and adjectives, thus:

*ob*, I                    *obs*, we
*oba*, of me (mine)        *obas*, of us, ours
*obe*, to me               *obes*, to us
*obi*, me                  *obis*, us

The indeterminate neuter termination is *os*.

The DEMONSTRATIVE and RELATIVE PRONOUNS are:

*at*, this (person)           *atos*, this (thing)
*et*, that (person)           *etos*, that (thing)
*kel*, who, which (person), (rel.).  *kelos*, which (thing).

POSSESSIVE PRONOUNS are formed from personal pronouns by suffixing the adjectival termination *ik*. They are subject to the same rules of syntax as other adjectives; *i.e.* they follow the noun; hence:

---

* The feminine prefix *ji* has been finally adopted at the Munich Congress of Volapükists, in August, 1887.

*obik*, my
*olik*, thy
*omik*, his *or* her (before a masc. noun)
*ofik*, her (before a fem. noun)
*obsik*, our
*olsik*, your
*omsik*, their (plural of *omik*)
*ofsik*, their (plural of *ofik*)

The genitival inflection *a* is also used in the formation of Compound Nouns; thus: *kukaneif*, kitchen knife; *julabuk*, school book.

The COMPARATIVE is formed by suffixing *um*, and the SUPERLATIVE by suffixing *ün*. The adverb terminates in *o*; thus:

|  | ADJECTIVE. | ADVERB. |
|---|---|---|
| POSITIVE | *gudik*, good | *gudiko*, good, well |
| COMPARATIVE | *gudikum*, better | *gudikumo*, better |
| SUPERLATIVE | *gudikün*, best | *gudiküno*, best. |

## VOCABULARY III.

*adelo*, to-day
*apod*, apple
*bad*, ill (noun)
*badlik*, bad (adj.)
*bäled*, age
*bäledik*, aged, old
*beatik*, blessed, happy, deceased
*bil*, beer
*blod*, brother
*bum*, the act of building
*bumot*, a building
*bumön*, to build
*bün*, pear
*cem*, a room
*deb*, debt
*del*, a day
*diso*, below, downstairs
*disik*, the lower
*fa*. from, on the part of
*fidön*, to eat, dine
*givön*, to give
*ibo*, because
*is*, here
*jiblod*, sister
*jidog*, bitch
*jikat*, cat (fem.)
*jinök*, aunt
*jönik*, beautiful
*kat*, cat generally, also
*klöd*, belief [tom-cat
*klödön*, to believe
*lif*, life
*lölik*, whole
*löpo*, above, upstairs
*löpik*, the upper
*mak*, a mark, the coin = one shilling
*malädik*, ill
*malädikel*, the patient (masc.)
*jimalädikel*, the patient (fem.) [*nus*
*masel*, master (Lat. *domi-*

*mekön*, to make
*mödik*, much
*nog*, as yet, still
*nök*, uncle
*plu ka*, more than
*si*, yes
*sibinön*, to exist, to be
*sis*, since
*smalik*, small
*spat*, a walk

*spatön*, to take a walk
*stök*, storey or floor (of a house)
*tim*, time
*us*, there
*viliko*, willingly, gladly
*vilön*, to will (Lat. *velle*)
*vin*, wine
*yun*, youth
*yunik*, young
*yunlik*, youthful

NUMERALS.

*bal*, one
*tel*, two
*kil*, three

*fol*, four
*lul*, five.

EXERCISE 3.

(*a*) Translate into English:

1. Yun binom tim jöniküu lifa lölik.
2. Blod olik löfom bili nog plu ka vini.
3. Kukel nöka obsik kukom bilasupi gudikum ka jikukel olsik.
4. Jiblods obik vilofs mekön adelo spati gletik ko mot olsik e ko ols.
5. Kelosi logon, atosi klödon; e klöd mekom beatik.
6. Bäled bumota at, keli logols is, binom gletikum ka klödon.
7. Logob sis dels tel us in gad jikati bäledik gadela olsik ko kats tel smalik.
8. Dom, keli bumamasel bumom obes, labom cemis mödikum ka olik, ibo cems lul gletik sibinoms in stök löpik e in stök disik cems fol smalikum, ab i jönik.
9. Jison jitidela olsik, kele dom et lönom, givof makis kil obe e maki bal jiblode obik.
10. Fidobs vilikumo apodis, ab viliküno bünis.
11. Blod omik yunikum labom debis badlik.
12. Mans at binoms nog yunlik, ab no ets.

(*b*) Translate into Volapük:

1. Our house is the largest.
2. I think so, but you also contract the worst

debts. (Say, "I believe it, but you (pl.) make also the worst debts.")

3. We (are going to) take a walk to-day with our mistress, whose brother you see yonder.

4. I give her the beautiful books, which belong to you (thee).

5. I hear that your (thy) younger sister is ill.

6. Yes, these (since) five days the sick (girl) does not go to school. (Say, "goes not to school.")

7. My aunt has three little dogs and a bitch; two of those dogs she will give to our huntsman.

8. The kitchen is on the top (uppermost) floor of yonder house, not in the lower (storey): the father has his room upstairs, and our old uncle below.

9. His mother will dine to-day in this little garden-saloon (garden-room).

10. Our architect (building-master, *bumamasel*) will not (does not intend, wills not) again build a school in his whole life.

11. Our cook (fem.) cooks wine-soup best, but she does not like to cook it. (Say, "she cooks it not willingly.")

12. I have four rooms upstairs and five downstairs.

§ 8.

A QUESTION is indicated by prefixing the particle *li* to the verb.

In sentences beginning with Interrogative Words or phrases, as *who? what? how much? how many?* the *li* is omitted.

If the subject in an interrogative sentence is a noun, it is placed before the verb; e.g., *fat li-binom gudik?* (is the father good?) In a truncated interrogative phrase, where the verb is not expressed, but only understood, the particle *li* is added to the most important word; thus: *li-Tom?* (is it Tom?); *Tom li-obsik?* (our Tom?); *li-si u li-no?* (yes or no?)

The DIMINUTIVE Suffix is *il*; thus: *bukil*, little book; *gadil*, little garden; *manil*, mannikin.

The DIMINUTIVE Particle *lu* expresses a reduction

B

of degree or of value, whilst the particle *le* expresses an enhancement of the same; thus:

hät, hat  
luhät, cap  
lehät, helmet  
jönik, beautiful  
lejönik, exceedingly beautiful  
fidön, to eat  

dom, house  
ludom, hut  
ledom, palace  
vomik, womanly  
luvomik, womanish, effeminate  
lufidön, to devour  

The Prefix *sma* (cf. *smalik*) expresses an object of the same category as the stem-word, but of lower degree; thus:

{ bim, tree  
{ smabim, shrub  
{ bed, bed  
{ smabed, nest  
{ zigad, cigar  
{ smazigad, cigarette  

## VOCABULARY IV.

ba,* an expletive, meaning "I wonder," as in *lilabol ba?* hast thou, I wonder? German, *hast Du wohl?*  
beno, good  
böd, bird  
but, boot  
danön, to thank (with accusative)  
glüg, church  
hetlik, ugly  
isik, of this place, belonging to this place  
in, in  
it, himself, herself  
jeval, horse  
jevalel, horse-soldier  
jipul, girl  
kim? (m), kif? (fem.), who?  

kis? what?  
kiom? (m.), kiof? (f.), kios? (n.), what?, which?  
kiplad? where?  
kostön, to cost  
läb, luck, fortune, happiness.  
läbik, lucky  
läd, lady  
lebeno, very good, very well  
lemön, to buy  
liko? how?  
limödik? how much?  
lödön, to dwell, inhabit  
monitön, to ride (on an animal)  
monitel, a rider  
mödik, much  
nulik, new  
ö! ahi! ah!  
plidön, to please  

---

\* *ba* also means perhaps.

*pük*, speech, language
*pükön*, to speak
*pul*, boy
*smokön*, to smoke
*so*, so
*söl*, master, sir, Mr.
*stadön*, to do (in "how do you do?") thus: *liko stadol?* how do you

do? French, *se porter;* German, *sich befinden.*
*stom*, weather
*su*, up, upon, on
*vol*, world
*volapük*, world-speech, universal language
*vedön*, to become
*zif*, town, city

NUMERALS (*continued*).
*mäl*, six        *vel*, seven

EXERCISE 4.

(*a*) Translate into English:
1. Deli gudik! Ö, li-nog in bed? Liko stadol, söl?
2. Danob oli, lebeno; e li-ol?
3. Li-vilol spatön adelo?
4. Stom li-binom ba jönik?
5. Kiplad buts obik binoms?
6. Li-logols jevali et, keli jevalel monitom?
7. Monitels li-plidoms ofe plu ka yagels?
8. Jiblods olik no li-golofs al glüg?
9. Kiplad lemon in zif isik hätis e luhätis gudikün?
10. Kisi jevals olsik mödik lufidoms?
11. Mens limödik pükoms volapüki?
12. Juleli kiom tidel lobom?

(*b*) Translate into Volapük:
1. Does this little-book belong to thee? Yes, or no?
2. Who does not like to go to church? (Say, "Who goes not willingly to church?")
3. Does not the teacher praise the industry of the boys? (Say, "Praises not the teacher?" etc.)
4. How much does your (thy) new hat cost? (Say, "How much costs?" etc.)
5. It costs six or seven marks; and yours (thine), madam?
6. Have not the horse-soldiers large helmets?
7. Anna is a very beautiful girl, and so womanly too. Is her sister Maggie also beautiful and womanly?

8. Maggie? Oh, no! she is effeminate and ugly.
9. The weather is getting (say, " becomes ") bad. Do you hear the thunder?
10. We see six birds'-nests on the trees of thy uncle's garden, and one on the shrub there.
11. Does your father smoke (say, " Smokes your father? " etc.) cigars or cigarettes?
12. What is happiness? Is he happier who lives in (inhabits) a palace, or he who inhabits a hut?

§ 9.
ON THE FORMATION OF TENSES.

All tenses (except the present) are formed by prefixes:

| | |
|---|---|
| *löfob*, I love | *ilöfob*, I had loved |
| *älöfob*, I loved | *olöfob*, I shall love |
| *elöfob*, I have loved | *ulöfob*, I shall have loved |

Nouns also are treated in a similar manner, thus; from *del*, day, are formed:
*adelo*, to-day    *odelo*, to-morrow
*ädelo*, yesterday    *udelo*, the day after to-
*edelo*, the day before yes-    morrow.
terday

Similarly, from *yel*, year, are formed:
*ayelo*, this year    *oyelo*, next year
*äyelo*, last year    *uyelo*, the year after next
*eyelo*, the year before last

Similarly from *mul*, month: *amulo*, *ämulo*, *emulo*, *omulo*, and *umulo*.

VOCABULARY V.

| | |
|---|---|
| *also*, well then | *Deutel*, (a) German |
| *Ägüpän*, Egypt | *deutik*, German (adj.) |
| *Ägüpänel*, Egyptian | *dünal*, a servant, minister |
| *bi*, because | *dünel*, a servant, porter |
| *bizugik*, excellent, most preferable | *Flent*, France |
| | *Flentel*, Frenchman |
| *bizugön*, to prefer | *flentik*, French (adj.) |
| *blinön*, to bring | *fit*, fish |
| *bötel*, waiter, butler | *foriko*, forthwith, immediately, anon |
| *des*, from…till | |
| *Deut*, Germany | *getön*, to receive, get |

*it*, self; German, *selbst;*
   French, *même*
*jidünel*, maidservant
*Jveizän*, Switzerland
*Jveizel*, a Swiss
*kaf*, coffee
*kiplada?* whence?
*kipladi?* whither?
*kömön*, to come
*läd*, lady, mistress
*län*, land
*lemasel*, great master
*liegik*, rich
*ludog*, wolf
*lufat*, step-father
*lupab*, caterpillar (cf. *pab*)
*Lusän*, Russia
*Lusänel*, (a) Russian
*lusänik*, Russian (adj.)
*mel*, sea
*menad*, humanity, mankind
*milagön*, to admire
*mödo*, much * (adv.)
*nebel*, valley
*Nelij*, England
*Nelijel*, Englishman
*nelijik*, English (adj.)
*no nog*, not yet
*pab*, butterfly
*pir*, pyramid
*plo*, for
*poed*, poetry, poesy
*poedel*, a poet
*poedal*, a great poet
*sagön*, to say
*se*, out, out of
*smacem*, small room, cabinet, boudoir
*snek*, snake
*snekafit*, eel
*söl*, sir, gentleman, Mr.
*sosus*, as soon as
*suno*, soon
*tävön*, to travel
*te*, only, not till
*tied*, tea
*valik*, all
*ven*, when, as (temporal)
*vob*, work
*vom*, woman
*vomül*, Miss, young lady

NUMERALS (*continued*).
*jöl*, eight      *zül*, nine

EXERCISE 5.

(*a*) Translate into English:

1. Göthe binom e obinom lemasel poeda deutik.
2. Blod olik li-emilagom glügabumis lejönik in Flent, Nelij e Lusän, ven ätävom us?
3. Dünan li-igivom ädelo bukis vome Robinson?
4. No, söl, no nog ugetom it omis.
5. Li-elogols piris Agüpäna?
6. Si, vomül, elogobs omis; esagon, das binoms bumots bäledikün menada, mödo bäledikum ka valiks deutik u nelijik.

---

* Instead of mödiko; the adverbial termination is often contracted by elision of the adjectival inflection *ik*.

7. Volapük li-ovedom pük vola lölik?
8. Kiplada äkömols? Kipladi golols?
9. Se lupab, keli älogols ädelo in gad obsik, pab ovedom suno, ba ya odelo.
10. Jibötel oblinof kafi ole foviko, sosun kukel ukukom omi.
11. Dünel John ogetom makis jöl u zül fa Nelijel liegik plo vob omik.
12. Sneks gletik no li-olufidoms fitis obsik?

(b) Translate into Volapük:

1. Egypt, says Herodotus, is the land of the Egyptians, thus only the valley of the Nile from Syene to the sea.
2. The maid has bought to-day eels for 8 marks; mother herself has told it me.
3. The Russians and the English will prefer tea, the French coffee, the Germans beer.
4. Where did the great poet live (say, "has the great poet lived") whom humanity admires?
5. The Russian had given me excellent cigarettes.
6. My step-father's house (say, "the house of my step-father") had in two storeys nine rooms, eight small rooms, and a kitchen.
7. As soon as you come (will have come) I will give you the three books of my uncle.
8. The waiter brought my brother wine; but he thanked (him) and went (away).
9. The French too have had great poets.
10. The Egyptian Cheops has built the greatest pyramid.
11. He did not come (say, "he came not") because he had not time.
12. The Swiss (pl.) whom we saw to-day spoke two languages—French and German, but not Russian.

## § 10.

ON THE FORMATION OF THE PASSIVE VOICE.

The Passive Voice is formed from the active voice by prefixing the letter *p* (in the present and in the infinitive, *pa*):

*palöfön*, to be loved   *palöfob*, I am loved
*päläfob*, I was loved   *pelöfob*, I have been loved
*pilöfob*, I had been loved   *polöfob*, I shall be loved
   *pulöfob*, I shall have been loved.

§ 11.

(a) RECAPITULATION OF NUMERALS.

Units:—*bal*, one   *fol*, four   *vel*, seven
   *tel*, two   *lul*, five   *jöl*, eight
   *kil*, three   *mäl*, six   *zül*, nine

(b) CONTINUATION OF NUMERALS.

The tens are formed from the units by the addition of *s*; thus:

   *bal*, one unit   *bals*, one ten = 10
   *tel*, two units   *tels*, two tens = 20
   *kil*, three units   *kils*, three tens = 30
   *zül*, nine units   *züls*, nine tens = 90

The tens precede the units. Thus we say, in Volapük, "twenty-one," and never "one-and-twenty."

   *balsebal* (*bals e bal*), ten and one = eleven
   *balsetel*, twelve
   *balsekil*, thirteen; and so on

Similarly:

   *telsebal*, twenty-one   *kilsetel*, thirty-two
      *folsekil*, forty-three; and so on
   *zülsezül*, ninety-nine   *mil*, a thousand
   *tum*, a hundred   *balion*, a million

§ 12.

The prefix *ne* always indicates the opposite notion of the word itself; thus:

   *bel*, mountain   *nebel*, valley
   *flen*, friend   *neflen*, foe
   *läbo*, luckily   *neläbo*, unluckily
   *labön*, to have   *nelabön*, to lack
   *mödiks*, many   *nemödiks*, few

If the word to be negatived begins with an *e*, the terminal *e* of the negative particle is elided; thus:

   *ek*, somebody   *nek*, nobody
   *egelo*, ever, always   *negelo*, never

## Vocabulary VI.

*al*, to
*äso*, as well as
*bif*, before (locally)
*büf*, before (temporally)
*bod*, bread
*de*, of, from
*desedön*, to send away
　(prefix *de* = away)
*delo*, by day
*dido*, indeed, certainly
*dlin*, a beverage
*dlinön*, to drink
*düp*, hour
*ek*, somebody
*fa*, of, from, by means of
*fagik*, distant, far
*fikulik*, difficult
*fot*, forest, wood
*fösefön*, to assure, asseverate
*funön*, to kill
*gedlanön*, to push back
　(prefix *ge* = back)
*Glik*, Greece
*Glikel*, (a) Greek
*gödel*, morning
*juk*, shoe
*ka*, than
*kanön*, inf. of "I can"
　(Lat., *posse*)
*kö*, where (relative)
*kodo*, on which account
　(relative)
*leyan*, gate (cf. *yan*)
*lovik*, soft, softly
*mat*, matrimony, married life
*matel*, husband
*mileg*, butter
*milig*, milk
*mit*, meat, flesh
*mütön*, inf. of "I must"
*neb*, near by, by the side of
*nefikulik*, easy (cf. *fikulik*)
*neit*, night
*neito*, at night
*nek*, nobody
*nen*, without (Lat. *sine*)
*nendas*, without that
*nu*, now
*ot*, the same
*pened*, a letter (Lat. *epistola*, not *litera*)
*penön*, to write
*pom*, fruit (Lat. *pomum*, not *frux*)
*pöfik*, poor
*Romel*, (a) Roman
*se*, out, out of
*sefön*, to secure, make safe
*skit*, leather
*tal*, earth
*ton*, (a) tone, sound
*tonod* (a) loud sound
*töbo*, hardly, with difficulty (Lat. *vix*)
*tu*, to, too
*valik*, all
*vemo*, very
*vendel*, evening
*vikod*, victory
*vikodön*, to conquer
*yan*, door
*yel*, year
*yuf*, help
*zendel*, midday
*zib*, food, viand

EXERCISE 6.
(a) Translate into English:
1. Juk at pemekom de skit bizugikün.
2. Kaf ko milig padlinom gödelo, mit pafidom zendelo, milegabod ko pom vendelo.
3. In düp bal peneds bals kanoms papenön fa nek.
4. Ton et binom tu lovik, kodo kanom palilön töbo bif cemayan.
5. Neito tonod egelo palilom läbo mödo fagikumo ka delo.
6. Dlin panelabom fa men fikulikumo, (fikulumo), zib ka.
7. Neläbo jimatel yagela 'pedlefof, nendas yuf äkanom pablinön ofe.
8. Dom flena obik su bel bif leyan pesefom büf yels balsezül plo maks folsmil.
9. Roma no pebumom in del bal.
10. Evikodobs dido, ab lultum obsikas pefunoms in pug bal.
11. Odelo zendelo neflens puvikodoms, e telmil foltum jöls omas pagedlanoms al zif.
12. Stägs balsekil päjutoms ädelo in fot obsik, e odelo nog mödikums ka tels pojutoms.

(b) Translate into Volapük:
1. Shoes and boots are made of (*de*) leather.
2. The earth is inhabited by more than 1,400 million men.
3. In two hours the enemies were conquered, and 775 of their men (men of them) were killed in the battle before the wood.
4. Will not the sound be heard on the mountain as well as in the valley?
5. Fifteen men with six hounds (hunting-dogs) have been seen at night in the orchard (fruit-garden) near the house of your (thy) friend.
6. Where they smoke (say, "one smokes") they also drink (say, "one also drinks").
7. The letter will be sent off to-morrow forthwith, as soon as it is written (as it shall have been written).
8. The Greeks were conquered by (*fa*) the Romans

but the Romans, even 2,000 years ago (say, "already before 2,000 years ") by the Germans.

9. The poor man lacks everything; he has hardly bread to eat; wherefore help must be rendered (brought) to him.

10. Only few houses could be built during (in) this year in our great town, which is now inhabited by 82,354 men.

11. By Russians, tea will always be preferred for supper, but not by Frenchmen.

12. Even to-day the Universal Language (Volapük) is spoken by more than 40,000 people (men).

§ 13.

The IMPERATIVE is formed by adding the termination, *öd;* thus:

*givolöd,* give (2nd person singular)
*givolsöd,* „ (2nd person plural)
*givobsöd,* let us give.

A milder form of the imperative is given by the termination *ös;* thus:

*givolös,* please to give
*golobsös,* let us go

§ 14.

Every cardinal number can be turned into a noun by adding *el,* and can be turned into a verb by adding *ön;* thus:

| CARDINAL. | NOUN. | VERB. |
|---|---|---|
| *tel,* two | *telel,* a pair | *telön,* to double |
| *kil,* three | *kilel,* a triplet | *kilön,* to treble |
| *lul,* five | *lulel,* a fiver | *lulön,* to quintuple |

A Cardinal is turned into an ORDINAL number by adding the suffix *id;* thus:

*balid,* the first   *telid,* the second   *kilid,* the third
and so on.

These are rendered adverbial by adding the suffix *o;* thus:

*balido,* firstly   *telido,* secondly   *kilido,* thirdly.

REPETITIVE Numerals are formed from cardinals or ordinals by adding the suffix *na*; thus:

*balsna*, ten times
*telsidna*, the twentieth time
*telsidno*, for the twentieth time

## VOCABULARY VII.

*alik*, every
*as sam (a.s.)* (e.g.), for example
*blibön*, to remain
*dil*, a part
*fatän*, fatherland
*foldil*, quarter, 4th part
*fögivön*, to forgive
*if*, if, when
*kimid?* the how-manieth?
*komip*, a combat, battle
*komipel*, a combatant
*komipön*, to fight
*laf*, half, noun (Fr. *moitié*)
*lanimälik*, bravely
*lenlilön*, to listen to
*liladön*, to read
*madik*, ripe
*nemödo*, a little (cf. *mödo*, voc. v.)
*paun*, lb. (also £)
*sätön*, to suffice, to be enough
*solat*, soldier
*timil*, moment
*timilo*, momentarily, for a moment
*tupön*, to disturb
*velat*, truth
*visit*, a visit
*visitön*, to visit
*yelatum*, century

## EXERCISE 7.

(a) Translate into English:

1. Binosöd! Men alik sagomöd velati.
2. Sagolsöd valikosi obe, kelosi elilols.
3. Solats valik komipomsöd lanimäliko plo fatän.
4. Kömolös nog adelo al obs!
5. Adelo no labob timi, binos ya düp velid e foldils kil.
6. Fösefob ole, das epenob penedi at ya zülna.
7. Fögivolsös, if tupob olis!
8. Deli kimid älabobs ädelo?
9. Älabobs kilsebalidi.
10. In tim ot solats ijutoms jölsevelidno.
11. Liladön balsna no nog sätom.
12. No fidolöd pomi, ibo balido no nog binom madik e telido no binol saunik.

(b) Translate into Volapük:

1. Let us go to-day into our beautiful forest.
2. Many towns have already been built for the second time, *e.g.* Rome.
3. I have told him a hundred times, that nobody will thank him for this.
4. One must fight bravely for the fatherland.
5. The Germans have conquered three times in the second half of this century: in the year eighteen hundred and sixty-four, in the year eighteen hundred and sixty-six, and in the years eighteen hundred and seventy and seventy-one.
6. I will not buy the house in the town, because, firstly, it costs four thousand five hundred pounds; and, secondly, I shall not remain here in England.
7. Read very industriously the book which you have received from (your) aunt.
8. What o'clock is it? (Say, "The how-manieth hour is it?")
9. It is already a quarter past eleven. (Say, "It is already hour eleven and one quarter.")
10. Please stop (remain) yet a moment, and promise us that you will dine with us to-morrow.
11. Kindly pardon me! I cannot to-morrow. We have a great hunt to-morrow.
12. There will be 9 or 10 English gentlemen with servants and dogs at the hunt.

§ 15.

The SUBJUNCTIVE is formed by adding the suffix -*la*\* to the corresponding tense of the indicative; thus:

| INDIC. | SUBJUNC. |
|---|---|
| *binom*, he is | *binomla*, he be, he may be |
| *äbinom*, he was | *äbinomla*, he might be |
| *ebinom*, he has been | *ebinomla*, he may have been |

---

\* The suffixes -*la* and -*öv*, being terminal syllables, are accented, see rule *c*, page 9. Accordingly we say *binomlá*, *äbinomöv*.

*ibinom*, he had been   *ibinomla*, he might have been

In the *obliqua oratio* (reported speech) the indicative is used with *das*, that; e.g., Asagom, das okömom, He said, that he would (will) come.

### § 16.

The CONDITIONAL is formed by adding the syllable -*öv*\* to the imperfect or pluperfect:

*äbinomöv*, he would be
*ibinomöv*, he would have been

MULTIPLICATIVE numerals are formed by adding the suffix *ik*, and those expressing classes or categories by the suffix *nik*; thus:

*bal*, one   *tum*, hundred
*balnik*, of one kind, simple   *tumnik*, a hundred sorts of

DISTRIBUTIVE numerals are expressed by placing the particle *a* before the word; thus:

*a jöl*, eight and eight, in sets of eight
*a jölna*, eight at a time, every eight times
*a jölid*, every eighth person

Similarly:

*a tel*, two at a time   *a telna*, every other time
*a telid*, every other person.

### VOCABULARY VIII.

*al*, to (with infinitive, expressing a purpose)
*ävendelo*, last evening
*can*, merchandise, wares, goods
*cil*, child
*dö*, of, concerning
*dunön*, to do
*e......e*, as well......as
*egelo*, always
*fatel*, grandfather
*filed*, conflagration
*gälod*, pleasure
*gödel*, morning
*if*, if
*kän*, cannon
*klig*, war
*kon*, narrative, story
*konön*, to narrate
*kösekön*, to sacrifice, devote
*labem*, property, wealth
*lif*, life
*lodam*, load, cargo
*lodön*, to load

---

\* *See* Note, p. 28.

*loned*, length
*lonedön*, to lengthen, protract
*malön*, to announce, indicate
*me*, with, by means of
*mon*, money
*naf*, ship
*nakömön*, to arrive
*nedön*, to need, want
*Nidän*, India
*pelön*, to pay
*pof*, haven, harbour
*pön*, penalty, punishment
*rivön*, to reach, attain
*savön*, to save, rescue, deliver
*spälik*, sparing, economical
*\*spälön*, to save, put by, economise

*stim*, honour, esteem
*stimön*, to honour, to esteem
*suäm*, price
*täv*, journey
*teat*, theatre
*tedel*, merchant
*tolad*, toll, custom, duty
*toladön*, to pay toll or duty
*toned*, ton, 1000 kilogs.
*ut*, he (dem. pron.)
*vadelo*, daily
*vipön*, to wish
*vob*, work
*vobel*, worker, workman
*vobön*, to work
*zeil*, goal
*zilik*, zealous

EXERCISE 8.

(*a*) Translate into English:

1. Ätävoböv al Jveiz, if älabobla moni.
2. Jiblod obik igolofōv al teat ävendelo, if no elabofla dunön tu mödikosi.
3. A lulid solatas pefunom, ibo teltum pefunoms de mil.
4. Sagon, das nedon kilnikosi al klig: moni, moni, e denu moni.
5. Äkonoböv tumnikosi dö tävs obik, if älabobla timi.
6. Tedel nelijik ipelomöv suämi kilik plo can, if te ikanomla getön omi.
7. Pauns fol imütomsöv papelön de toned as pön, if lodam nafa no pitoladomla.
8. Pajutos kilna in zif obsik ko kän al malön filedi.
9. Julels ämütomsöv telön duti omsik, if ävilomsla rivön zeili.

---

\* Cf. *spälön* and *savön*.

10. Binolöd spälik, e otelol labemi olik in yels nemödik.
11. If fat e fatel obsik no ispälomsla so ziliko, no äbinobsöv mens so liegik.
12. Vipob, das naf obsik ko lodam gletik de Nidän ya cnakömomla in pof.

(*b*) Translate into Volapük:

1. I would lengthen my letter; but the longest letters are not always the best.
2. She would daily go to the theatre with her friend (fem.) if she had money as well as time.
3. His uncle would travel to London, if he had not threefold work to do.
4. My friend told me that not one apple in six (not every sixth apple) of the largest apple-tree in his orchard was ripe yet.
5. With the greatest pleasure I would call upon (visit) your aunt, if she were at home.
6. It would be an honour to the brave combatants to be killed for the fatherland.
7. Would the ship have so soon reached (arrived in) port, if she had had a double cargo?
8. The enemy daily shot twice with cannon, in the morning and in the evening, but hardly one man in nine (the ninth man) of our soldiers was hit.
9. How many pounds would you need for the journey?
10. The ship had a very mixed cargo on board (say "had loaded a thousand different kinds of things"), and the duty on most of the goods had been doubled in that year.
11. They could be saved fourteen at a time.
12. Honour those who readily (forthwith) would sacrifice their lives for their brothers.

### § 17.

Every PARTICIPLE terminates in *öl*:

*givöl*, giving
*egivöl*, having given
*stimöl*, honouring
*pastimöl*, being honoured
*pestimöl*, having been honoured

REFLECTIVE VERBS are formed with the reflective pronouns *obi, oli, oki, obis, olis, okis* (accusative), *obe, ole, oke, obes, oles, okes* (dative); thus:

*löfob obi*, I love myself
*löfol oli*, thou lovest thyself
*löfom oki*, he loves himself
*löfof oki*, she loves herself
*löfos oki*, it loves itself
*löfobs obis*, we love ourselves
*löfols olis*, you love yourselves
*löfoms okis,* } they love themselves
*löfofs okis,*
*ok*, French *se* and German *sich*

It is needful carefully to distinguish between reflective and reciprocal action of a verb; thus:

They love themselves, *löfoms okis;* but
They love each other, *löfoms balvoto**

Similarly with possessive pronouns of the third person, distinction must be made between "his" and "her," referring to the subject or to another person, like *suus* and *eius*, in Latin. Only in the first can *okik* be employed; thus:

*labom buki okik*, he has his (own) book
*labom buki omik*, he has his (another's) book

### VOCABULARY IX.

*adelo*, to-day
*äs*, as
*banön*, to bathe
*blim*, equipment, dowry
*cin*, machine
*dalebön*, to lack, need, suffer from want, starve
*deilön*, to die, decease
*delidik*, dear, expensive
*difik*, different
*dledön*, to fear, dread
*dub*, through, by means of
*fil*, fire
*filedön*, to burn
*fizir*, officer
*flapön*, to beat
*flum*, river
*gälön*, to rejoice
*jol*, coast
*kapälön*, to understand
*kösel*, cousin (m.)
*lak*, lake
*len*, at, to, by          now)
*lenu*, forthwith (from *nu*,

---

* *Balvoto*, contracted form of *balvotiko* (from *bal*, one, and *votik*, other).

*mel*, sea
*matapömetön*, to betroth (cf. *pömetön*)
*migön*, to mix
*mufön*, to move
*nam*, hand
*nil*, proximity, nearness
*nilik*, near (adv.)
*nilel*, neighbour
*nilön*, to approach (with Accve.)
*nilü*, near, nigh
*ninflumön*, to flow into, to terminate (said of a river)
*numön*, to count

*pömetön*, to promise
*sevokön*, to exclaim
*sol*, sun
*spidön*, to hasten
*stem*, steam
*stun*, astonishment
*sumön*, to take
*sugiv*, task, exercise
*tulön*, to turn
*us*, yonder, there
*vat*, water
*velatik*, true
*vemo*, very much, greatly
*vunön*, to wound
*xab*, axle, axis
*zü*, round, about

EXERCISE 9.

(*a*) Translate into English:

1. Tal tulom in düps telsefol zü xab okik e in dels kiltum mälselul e foldil bal zü sol.
2. Cins et pamufoms dub stem.
3. Cinavobel obsik eflapom su nam; elogob it nami pevunöl omik.
4. Spidöl se dom filedöl äsevokom: Savamöd oki kel kanom.
5. Cil efiledöl oki dledom fili.
6. Ägälom oki vemo, ven äsagob ome, das okömol nog adelo.
7. No kapälobs balvoto.
8. No vunolsöd olis dub neifs gletik.
9. Sis dels jöl banobs (obis) in flum u in lak ko sons flena obsik edeilöl.
10. Len jol mela vat flumas migom oki ko vat mela.
11. Nilel obsik bumom domi jönik oke.
12. Kösel obik ematapömetom oki ko vomül Anna jikösel olik.

(*b*) Translate into Volapük:

1. Like (as) the earth, so also the sun turns on his axis.

c

2. Cooked meat is wholesomer than raw (not cooked).
3. The defeated enemies approached our town.
4. We prefer wine mixed with water to unmixed wine.
5. My sister went up (say "approached") the dying (woman) and gave her her (say "the") hand.
6. Here the nearest neighbours do not understand each other, because they speak different languages.
7. To conquer oneself is the most beautiful victory.
8. Starving men do not work well.
9. The astonishment of the people (of the men) was great, when they saw the rescued man near the coast.
10. Not all river water readily (say "forthwith") mixes with sea water.
11. Is it true that thy friend (fem.) is betrothed to the young officer?
12. Yes, she will soon purchase her trousseau (equipment).

## § 18.

The NAMES of the SEASONS are compounds of *tim*, time:

*flolatim*, spring (*flol*, flower)
*hitatim*, summer (*hit*, heat)
*flukatim*, autumn (*fluk*, fruit)
*nifatim*, winter (*nif*, snow)

The NAMES of the MONTHS end in *ul*, (*mul*, month, allied to *mun*, moon), and are expressed in sequence by the ordinal numbers.

*balul*, January     *relul*, July
*telul*, February     *jölul*, August
*kilul*, March     *zülul*, September
*folul*, April     *balsul*, October
*lulul*, May     *balsebalul*, November
*mälul*, June     *balsetelul*, December

The DAYS of the WEEK naturally end in *del*, day, and their names also are formed with ordinal numbers, inserting the vowel *ü*.

*balüdel*, Sunday  *folüdel*, Wednesday
*telüdel*, Monday  *lulüdel*, Thursday
*kilüdel*, Tuesday  *mälüdel*, Friday
*relüdel*, Saturday

ADVERBS of TIME are formed from the days of the week in the usual manner by adding the suffix *o*; as:

*balüdelo*, o' Sundays, etc.
cf. *adelo, vendelo*, etc.

The NAMES of the SCIENCES end in *av*:
*gitav*, jurisprudence (*git*, right, just)
*gletav*, mathematics (*glet*, magnitude)
*godav*, theology (*God*, God)
*medinav*, medical science (*medin*, medicine)
*minav*, mineralogy (*min*, mineral)
*natav*, natural science (*nat*, nature)
*nimav*, zoology (*nim*, animal)
*planav*, botany (*plan*, plant)
*pükav*, philology (*pük*, speech)
*sapav*, philosophy (*sap*, wisdom)
*talav*, geology (*tal*, earth)
*tikav*, logic (*tik*, thought; *tikön*, to think)

Some sciences, however, retain their common names almost unchanged; thus: *füsüd*, physics; *kiem*, chemistry; *filosop*, philosophy.

The termination *äl* indicates something mental or spiritual:

*tikäl*, spirit  *kapäl*, intelligence (*kap*, head)

The terminations *ed* and *am*, like our "-ing," signify a state or an activity; thus:

From *fin*, end, is formed *finam*, termination
„ *glet*, magnitude, is formed *gletam*, increase, enlargement, expansion
„ *nindilön*, to classify, is formed *nindilam*, classification
„ *tik*, thought, is formed *tikam*, consideration
„ *lab*, have, is formed *labed*, possession
„ *tak*, rest, is formed *taked*, repose
„ *tal*, earth, is formed *taled*, geography

## § 19.

The terminations *-ef* and *-ad* signify a collection of persons, a corporate body; thus:

From *Krit*, Christ, is formed *kritef*,* Christendom
„ *men*, man (Lat. *homo*), is formed *menad*, humanity, the human family

The English *for-* in "forgive," *per-* in "persecute," *par-* in "pardon," *pur-* in "pursue," are rendered in Volapük by *fe-* (occasionally by *fö-*), and the English *a-* in "awake," "await," and *e-* in "espy" are rendered in Volapük by *da-*; thus:

From *litön*, to give light, is formed *dalitön*, to light up, illumine
„ *logön*, to see, is formed *dalogön*, to catch sight of, espy
„ *tuvön*, to find, is formed *datuvön*, to invent, discover
„ *vestigön*, to search, investigate, is formed *davestigön*, to find out by searching

Thus, in "Search the scriptures," we should use *davestigön*.

From *yebön*, to use, is formed *fegebön*, to use up, consume
„ *givön*, to give, is formed *fögivön*, to forgive, pardon
„ *golön*, to go, is formed *fegolön*, to pass away, elapse, perish

PROPER NOUNS are not declined. The genitive is expressed by the preposition *de*, the dative by the preposition *al*, and the accusative is distinguished from the nominative by its position in the sentence.

### VOCABULARY X.

†*as*, as
*äyelo*, last year
*balüdo*, first, at first
*begin*, beginning, commencement
*beginön*, to begin

---

\* N.B.—*Kritar* is Christianity, the system of Christ; but *kritef* is Christendom.

† Cf. *Äs* (voc. ix.) with *as*. *Äs* expresses similarity; *as*, identity; thus: *pükom äs tidel*, he speaks as (though he were a teacher; *pükom as tidel*, he speaks as (being) a teacher.

*belem*, mountain range
*bepenön*, to describe
*dabalik*, singly
*dalön*, to allow, permit
*danön*, to thank, be indebted for
*deil*, death
*deilön*, to die
*dil*, (a) part
*do*, although
*fedugön*, to mislead, seduce
*gab*, earl, count
*geilik*, high
*gladajuk*, skate (*glad*, ice; *juk*, shoe)
*gladajukön*, to skate
*gün*, gun
*günapur*, gunpowder (see *pur*)
*jü*, till
*kaled*, calendar, almanac
*kalön*, to calculate, reckon
*kapälüb*, intelligence
*kod*, cause
*kritik*, Christian
*lafayel*, half-year
*legivot*, (a) present
*lieg*, riches, wealth
*liegik*, rich, wealthy
*liköf*, constitution, nature of thing
*lugivön*, to lend
*mödo*, much (adverbially)
*nemön*, to name
*nevelo*, never
*nifön*, to snow
*niver*, university
*nol*, knowledge, science
*nolik*, scientific
*nonik*, no, none (adjve.)
*Nugän*, Hungary

*num*, number
*numön*, to count
*ofen*, often
*ovi*, over
*panemön*, to be called, named
*pesevo*, admittedly (*sevon*, to know; Fr. *connaître*, G. *kennen*)
*plofed*, professor
*plökön*, to pluck
*pöf*, poverty
*pöfik*, poor
*pur*, powder
*segun*, according
*senön*, to feel
*slip*, sleep
*smilön*, to laugh
*stab*, foundation, bottom
*stabiko*, fundamentally thoroughly
*studel*, a student
*studön*, to study
*stunön*, to be astounded, wonder, admire
*sudm*, sum, price
*sudmön*, to amount
*suemön*, to comprehend
*sükön*, to seek
*taked*, repose (noun)
*takedön*, to repose
*te*, only, not till
*tif*, theft
*valemo*, generally
*valiko*, in general
*ved*, origin
*veütik*, weighty, important
*vig*, week
*votik*, other

Exercise 10.

(a) Translate into English:
1. Vig nonig fegolom nen vob: e telüdelo e lulüdelo labobs dunön in gad, kilüdelo, folüdelo, mälüdelo e velüdelo vobobs domo; te balüdelo takedön padalos obes.
2. Yel panindilom in yelatims fol e yelatim alik in muls kil.
3. Nifatim beginom ko begin balsetelula, flolatim ko kilul, hitatim ko mälul, flukatim ko zülul.
4. Nindilam kaleda binom votik, ibo segun kaled kalobs a. s. hitatimi sis mälul telsebalid jü zülul telsekilid, do hit ofen vedom gletik ya in mälulavig balid e stom vedom flukatimik ya sis begin zülula.
5. Charles elugivom buki de Francis, keli at igetom as legivot fa tidel okik äyelo al William.
6. Taled bepenom tali; taled nolik davestigom kodis liköfa tala valemo e länas dabalik, talav binom stab taleda, ibo davestigom vedi tala e länas.
7. Sol dalitom tali e muni.
8. Nök omik binom plofed medinava.
9. Niver obsik labom godavelis mödo mödikum ka gitavelis in lafayel at.
10. Kisi natavels studoms?
11. Studoms füsüdi e kiemi, minavi, planavi e nimavi; studoms i gletavi, ibo nen kapälüb kela natav no kanom pasuemön stabiko.
12. Tikäl mena nedom e dagetom takedi dub slip

(b) Translate into Volapük:
1. Christianity does not yet comprise one quarter of the human family.
2. When Alfred beheld Edward, he said laughingly, "Your friend is a good fellow (*men*), but he will not set the Thames on fire." (Say, "He has not invented gunpowder.")
3. Pardon me, sir, that I did not come yesterday; I had wholly forgotten the hour on Thursday.
4. Logic is a part of philosophy.
5. Does your brother study philology or mathematics?

6. Our university has never had so many students of theology as in this half-year.

7. Only in our time has it been possible to study thoroughly the nature of the sun.

8. Since April of this year I have used up all my money.

9. It snows in winter, and people skate; in spring one plucks flowers.

10. Those rich earls have large possessions in Hungary.

11. This poor workman has been driven to (seduced into) theft by poverty.

12. The steam-engine (steam-machine) is indeed the most important invention of our century; we owe (*danön*) it to an Englishman.

### § 20.

From *top* (place) are derived the terminations *op* for the five quarters of the globe, and *öp* for other ocalities:

*Yulop*, Europe
*Silop*, Asia
*Fikop*, Africa
*Melop*, America
*Talop*, Australia
*lotöp*, inn, hotel (*lot*, guest)

*bilöp*, alehouse (*bil*, beer)
*valadöp*, waiting room (*valadön*, to wait)
*kiöp?* where?
*zümöp*, environs (*züm*, circle)

From *län* (land) is derived the termination *än*, added to the names of most countries:

*Cinän*, China
*Täl* or *Tälän*, Italy
*Spän*, Spain
*Beljän*, Belgium
*Bayän*, Bavaria

*Saxän*, Saxony
*Jlesän*, Silesia
*Türän*, Thuringia
*Nelijän*, England

The cardinal points terminate in *üd*:

*nolüd*, north
*sulüd*, south

*lefüd*, east
*resüd*, west

The names of animals mostly (but not always) terminate in *af;* e.g. *foxaf,* fox; but *lep,* ape, monkey.

The termination *üp,* derived from *düp,* hour, expresses time:

*lifüp,* a lifetime (*lif,* life)
*tidüp,* course of study; but, *tidadüp,* lesson, hour's teaching (*tidön,* to teach)
*kiüp?* when? at what time?

The termination *em* expresses a collection of things, and *öm* a collection of tools, utensils.

*belem,* a mountain range (*bel,* mountain)
*domöm,* house-gear
*gadöm,* garden tools
*feilöm,* agricultural implements (*feil,* acre)

The termination *en* indicates a trade, workshop, or manufacture, as our *ery* in brewery.

*taben,* carpentery, from *tab,* table
*baken,* bakery ,, *bakön,* to bake

The terminations *ug* and *öf* are our *-ness* in "darkness":

*binug,* essence (*bin,* being, Lat. *esse*)
*dulöf,* durability (*dul,* duration)
*flenöf,* friendliness
*stanöf,* constancy (*stan,* stand)

The termination *ö* is used in exclamations, as in

*bafö!* bravo! *spidö!* be quick! (*spid,* speed)

The termination *ü* is used with some prepositions, as in

*nilü,* near by *demü,* on account of

The prefix *ge-,* like our *re-,* expresses "back":

*geregön,* to travel back
*gesagön,* to reply
*gegivön,* to give back, return

The prefix *di-,* like the Latin *dis-* or *di-,* expresses "asunder," "in pieces."

*diblekön,* to shiver (*blek,* fracture)
*distukön,* to pull down, destroy (*stuk,* edifice, structure)

## Vocabulary XI.

*abu*, per contra, on the other hand (L. *autem*)
*äl*, towards
*anik*, any, a few
*bel*, mountain
*büfo*, before (temporal)
*caf*, kettle
*datürön*, to discover
*dis*, under
*dol*, pain
*du*, whilst (temporal)
*dunik*, active
*filabel*, volcano (fire mountain)
*fimän*, continent (large mass of land)
*foginel*, foreigner
*fut*, foot
*futel*, pedestrian
*futelön*, to walk, go on foot
*geilik*, high
*glät*, glass
*glätik*, made of glass
*glebelem*, chief mountain range
*gletam*, growth, expansion
*glezif*, chief town, capital
*kam* (a) plain
*kinän*, kingdom, empire
*lapin*, prey, booty
*lebalik*, unique
*lel*, iron
*lelod*, railway
*lot*, guest
*lotug*, inn, hostelry, hotel
*lovemelik*, beyond the sea, transoceanic
*domöm taimik*, earthenware
*mated*, wedding, marriage
*meditön*, to meditate, consider, think
*met*, metre (39·37 in.)
*Nelij*, England
*ni......ni* = neither......nor
*nim*, animal
*ninlödel*, inhabitant
*ove*, over
*pag*, village
*pakön*, to spread
*plä*, except
*plö*, outside
*plös*, therefor, for it
*pükat*, speech
*sak*, sack, bag, purse
*seistön*, to lie, be situated
*setenön*, to extend, to stretch (of mountains)
*sotimo*, at times
*stunik*, astonishing
*sufön*, to suffer
*süt*, street
*taim*, clay
*teldik*, many a one
*tudunön*, to exaggerate
*vayeliko*, yearly
*vid*, width
*röbön*, to acquire

### Exercise 11.

(*a*) Translate into English:

1. In Talop ni leps ni foxafs sibinoms, valemo lapinanims nonik, ab in taladils votik i no sibinoms sakanims Talopa plä aniks nemödik in Melop.

2. London binom glezif Nelija; seistom in lefüd Nelija.

3. Stettin seistom nolülefüdo des Berlin, Leipzig abu sulüvesüdo.

4. Lifüp menas li-evedom lonedikum in yelatum obsik?

5. Feilöm Nolümelopelas binom mödo gudikum ka ut Yulopelas.

6. No binos velatik, das Nelij seistom dis vid nolüdikum ka Nolüdeut.

7. Spidö! Mütoms gevegön, büfo neit beginom.

8. No li-milagols stanöfi, dub kel jimalädikel sufof dolis okik?

9. Läds e jipuls egevegoms dub lelod, abu obs egefutelobs ko puls.

10. Cato äfinom pükati alik sagöl: Carthago mütom padistukön.

11. In süt kiom tabens e bakens mödikün sibinoms is?

12. Belems Späna binoms mödo geilikum ka uts Jlesüna u Saxäna, Deuta valemo u Nelija.

(b) Translate into Volapük:

1. The chief ranges of America stretch (setenön) North to South: those of Asia, East to West.

2. The highest mountains of South America are volcanoes.

3. The capital of Bavaria lies 500 metres above the sea; that of Spain, 600.

4. When did Columbus discover America? In the month of October of the year 1492.

5. Thanks to the kindness of thy uncle, that in that bad weather I found a place of shelter (slupöp) in the nearest inn.

6. The pupils sometimes answer the teacher without considering.

7. In many German towns and villages people are still wont to smash crockery and glass before the door on the evening preceding the wedding.

8. The Thuringian forest is visited yearly by a great number of foreigners.

9. The growth since last century of the transoceanic colonies (possessions) of Great Britain is astonishing.
10. The German empire acquired its greatest transoceanic colony in East Africa.
11. Vesuvius of Italy is the only active volcano of the European continent.
12. China has more inhabitants than all Europe.

## PÜKOTS.

### Lä Visit.

1. Deli gudik, söl!
2. Vekömö, flen! Siadolös oli!
3. Liko stadol?
4. Lebeno.
5. Liko panemol?
6. Kiplad lödol?
7. Lödob in Beljän.
8. Se zif kiom binol motöfik?
9. Brüssel binom motöfazif obik.
10. Paels olik li-lifoms nog?
11. Lifayelis limödik labol?
12. Labob lifayelis telselul.
13. Jinol labön lifayelis mödikum.
14. Li-tävol ya lonedo in Deut?
15. No, söl; emotävob te büf dels kil de Brüssel.
16. Adyö! Visitolös obi suno denu!

### Dö Stom.

1. Stom binom jönik adelo.
2. Sol litom ya sis gödel; binos lesumiko vamik.
3. Binos ni tu vamik ni tu kalodik.
4. Deno binos flukatimik; gödels e vendels binoms ya lukalodik.
5. Vedos nu glumik.
6. Klödob, das olömibos odelo.
7. Li-elilol tötön?
8. Eflcdos ädelo, ab no enifos; sil äblibom klülik.

## Dö Teat e Musig.

1. Li-ebinol ya in teat nulik obsik?
2. Si, läd, äbinob us büf vig bal; li-ol i?
3. Teatapled kimik papledom adelo, yofapled u lügapled?
4. Vipob logön damatelami lekanitelas de Richard Wagner.
5. Kisi cedol dö lop at?
6. Musig binom lejönik.
7. Li-elilol ya jikaniteli nulik?
8. Teat obsik labom egelo damatelis sikikün.
9. Jiblod olik li-binof jilöfan musiga?
10. Si, vomül kanitof i lebeno.
11. Li-ogeton nog bilieti plo konzed odelik?

## Dö Fidön.

1. Kipladi golol so spido?
2. Vilob golön al staud al fidön.
3. Vipob pötiti gudik ole.
4. Danob, ab pötüt obik no obinom gletik, bi scnob malädik.
5. Vokolöd böteli!
6. Kisi dälob blinön ole, söl?
7. Givolöd obe pori loeta e gläti vina ledik.
8. Löfob vemo fidön glünedi flifik.
9. Li-vipol i milegi e fömadi al postab?
10. Lesi; ga stopö! No blinolöd postabi, binos ya tu lato, mütobs golön al dom.
11. Dlinobsös al leläb balvoto!

## Lä Tedel.

1. Vipob gödeli gudik ole, söl. Dini kimik vilol lemön?
2. Vipob lemön stofi plo blit e blötaklot.
3. Limödo met klöfa blägik at kostom?
4. Makis telsefol.
5 Li-vo? Atos binos mödo tu delidik.
6. Dabegob miglamis tel juega.
7. Eko mon plo can!
8. Adyö, söl; begob bestimön obis i fälo.

Dö Tävön.
1. Milmets limödik binoms de is al zif nilikün?
2. Leils bals, also milmets velsefol.
3. Veg li-binom gudik plo futel?
4. Nö; veg dugom da fot gletik e ovi flums ko pons badik.
5. Süt li-binom nesefik?
6. O no, lilon nosi dö lapinels.
7. No binos valiko pöligik, ni delo ni neito.
8. Vegi kimik müton vegön?
9. Sosus ukömol su bel, flekolöd deto e tün, ven urivol flumi, nedeto.
10. Otuvol i adelo menis sätik su länasüt, bi labobs zeladeli.
11. Dani ladlik!
12. Vipob tävi läbik ole!

## KONS.

### 1.

Ven ek äsäkom filosopele Thales, kis binos tugedik menes valik, ägesagom: "Spel, ibo i mens et laboms ati, kels laboms lenosi votik."

### 2.

Spartänels äbinoms valöpo pesevik du gesags blefik e dlelföl okik. Ven ek äsäkom rege spartänik Agis, solatis limödik älabom, äsagom: "So mödikis äs zesüdoms al vikodön neflenis."

### 3.

Nilü zifaleyan man ästanom e älubegom. Söl sembal, kel äbeigolom, äsäkom ome, kikod lubegom. "O söl löfik!" lubegel äsagom, "neläb gletik esüpitom obi: büf dels nemödik domil obik ko lab valik pedefiledom." "Li-labol zepami de löpöf olik das elabol neläbi at?" söl äsäkom. "Liedö," lubegel ägesagom, "pedefiledom ko pliems lemänik."

### 4.

Ven sanel mäkabik äseistom su deilabed, flens omik äsäkoms ome, sanele kiom äkanomsöv konfidön okis, if ämalädomsla. "Onemob sanelis kil bizugik oles," sanel deilöl äsagom, "fe sevols valik omis, ab ekonsidols omis jünu nemödo. Panemoms: malöf, vat e spatön ofen in but libik."

5.

"Kisi dukol is su vab?" toladal äsäkom feilele, kel äbeivegom lä toladadom. "Zabi," feilel älovopükom toladale al lil. "No li-kanol sagön osi kleiliko," toladal äsügom, "if binos nos votik?" "Flen löfik," feilel ägesagom, "jevals obik getoms te selediko zabi; ab if äplakomsla, das dukob zabi so mödik, ästadoböv badiko!"

6.

Yunel, kel änevelatom kösömo, äkonom vöno in sog dö tävs okik e de makabs, kelis elogom. Bevü votikos äkonom i sukölosi: "Su täv oba lätik äkömob al zif, in nil kela lek som sibinom, das gegivom vödi zülsezülna." Söl, keli nevelatön nejemik mena at äskanom ya lonedo, äsagom foviko: "Atos binos smalöf velatik! Labob leki mödo jönikum su gued obik. If tlidob se dom gödelo, vokob: gödeli gudik, lek! E gesagom foviko: Danob, söl benik!" Sog lölik äbeginom smilön, e sagon, das yunel et no fälo nevelatom siso so nejemiko.

7.

In pag Nugäna glügakosek äbinom. Musigel, kel ipledom bäfaviolini in lotöp, ägolom latiko in neit al dom e äpolom bäfaviolini okik su bäk. Ven ägolom da fot, ludogs jöl äkoskömoms ome e äletoms senitön kleiliko desäni oksik ome. Fug äbinom nemögik, i tasteifam alik ibinomöv vanlik. Musigel no äsüenom lonedo, ädasumom bäfaviolini okik, äpladom oki zenodü süt e äbeginom to tlep oka gletik pledön lenämiko su bäfaviolin okik. Ludogs äbinoms pejeköl, e bi no änoloms, tuvemaf kimik äbinom din, kel ädibatonom so mekadiko, ämogonoms.

8.

Lein, kel äbinom ya bäledik e no älabom nämis

sätik al kanön yagön, ädatikom käfi al lukijafön nulüdi oke. Asimulom maladi. Nims fota äkömoms al visitön regi oksik, ab pädimidoms e pälufidoms fa lein. Fino i foxaf äkömom al lein, yed äblibom bif ninavag leina e no ävilom nitlidön, do lein äsuflagom omi alos. Sikod lein äsäkom, kikod no ävilom nitlidön? Foxaf käfik ägesagom: " Bi logob futavegedis nimas mödik, kels egoloms al ninavag, ab futavegedis nonik nimas, kels igoloms se ninovag."

9.

Tedel, kel äkösömom polön sali al zif nilelik dub mucuks okik, ämütom egelo stepön da flum du tävam at. Ven ästepom da flum balna denu, mucuk äseslifom fädiko e älefalom ko fled okik. Sal ädiflumom dilo in vat, e mucuk sustanöl äsenitom, das fled okik ivedom leitikum. Ven ägolom da flum denu pos tim anik, äbäjedom oki desäno e nena dub flaps äkanom pastigön sustanön. Tedel, kel pädämom dub atos levemo, äkonom osi nilele okik, e at äkonsälom ome, suseitön spogis e laini mucuke e täno dukön omi da flum. Sosus mucuk äkömom al flum, äbäjedom oki denu, ab atna al däm okik, ibo spogs e lain äfuloms okis ko vat e fled äbinom nu luüno telna so vetik. Siso, sagon, mucuk eseslifom nevelo in flum denu.

10.

Abinos büf yels plu ka tum, ven Göthe ävisitom ofen Türänafoti, dilo al sulogön meinöpis usik ledükäna Saxän-Weimar, kela dünal äbinom, dilo al yagön ko ledük Karl August, gleflen okik, dilo al studön belemanati e planavoli belema lejönik, juitöl leigüpo venudis läna. Du del teldik ädutevom belis e nebelis, pato in zümöp de Ilmenau, e du neit teldik äslipom su letuigs glünik peinas türänik in yagaludom lutik. Balna vendel äsüpitom omi zenodü fot su geil nilü Ilmenau panemöl Gickelhahn, mäkabik demü lukilogam jönik ovi belem pefotöl. Sol ädisom in mayed stilik äl vesüd, püd zelik vendela züluhlik äpakom oki ovi topöf. Poedal älelogom devodiko deli deilöl e nati flukatimik, kodöl luladäli. In ladälod at äpenom me stib su völ ludoma boadik, keli legeil bela äpolom, liänis at:

>Ove geils valik
>   binom taked,
>in bimaklons valik
>   töbo senol
>blädi bal;
>bödils seiloms in fot;
>valadolöd ga, suno
>takedol i ol.

Ti pos yelatum lafik in tim motöfadela okik lätik poedal bäledanik äsükom geili lesumik nog balna. Äbetlidom ludomi et, kö istebom du düps läbik so mödik ko plin okik, nu ya edeilöl, e ko flens löfik votik. Su völ liens pepenöl in tim et ästanoms nog. Göthe ämütom dlenön, e neluimöl dlenis ädenuom vödis lätik:

>"Valadolöd ga, suno
>takedol i ol!"

Vo äbinos lätikna, das ävisitom beli. Muls nemödik täno äslipom slipi tenalik.

## SPOD.*

### 1.

DANOTAPENED

Paris, Place Malesherbes, 108,
*balul,* 1*id,* 1887.

*Söle J. J., Liverpool.*

Söl löfik,
 Labob soni keli vipob sedön al zif olik, dat lenadom plobo püki nelijik.
 Äbinob-öv vemo kotenik, if äkanol-la lasumön omi in tedadom olik: älenadom-öv otüpo püki e tedi.
 Son obik labom yelis balsejöl, binom vemo dutik sevom bukami e penom nepöko pükis fleutik e tälik Valadob gepüki sunik, e blibo, Söl löfik,
  dünan olik divodikün,
   N. N.

### 2.

ZÜLAG.—LEBLIMAM STITA LEBÖBA.

Bordeaux, *telul* 5*id,* 1887.

S.,
 Labob stimi nunön oli, dub zülag at, das eleblimob in zif at stiti leböba e komitäta laböl plo fiam.
   C. D.
 Begob oli noetön disapenedi obik e bestimön obi suno ko komits olik.

---

* This correspondence is, with the author's kind permission, taken from Professor Pflaumer's *Vollständiger Lehrgang des Volapük.*

3.

FÜNAM DUNANÄTA VALIKODIK.

Berlin, *kilul*, 10*id*, 1887.

Söl,

Melak obsik ko län olik evedom vemo pesetenöl sis yels anik. Edanemobs sikodo söli D. in Odessa, as dunani obsik valikodik plo Lusän lölik.

Egivobs ome dalami lensumön komitis plo kal obsik e kitön pelamis in nem obsik.

Otuvol diso disapenedi söla D.

Spelobs das ogebol vemo ofen medami omik plo bonedams olik.

Dünans olik,

F. K. & Ko.

4.

DANOTAPENED.

Stockholm, *folul* 30*id*, 1887.

*Söles F. & Ko., Paris.*

Egetobs bonedami de francs 10,000 de söls L. & Ch. in Orleans. Bi leno sevobs sölis at, begobs olis vestigön va juitoms klödati mödik in zif omsik.

Pömetobs biseo oles das ogebobs kautiko nünis olsik, e lesagobs oles das obinos gälod gletik plo obs, ven okanobs duinön oles in zit sümik.

Binobs dünans olsik divodikün,

K. & P.

5.

GEPÜK.

Paris, *lulul*, 8*id*, 1887.

*Söles K. & P., Stockholm.*

No kanobs givön oles nünis fümik dö tedadom, penömodöl in pened olsik de 30*id*, mula büfik.

Söls L & Ch. laboms lemacemi gletik in süt jönikün zifa, ab nolobs nosi tefü monameds omsik.

Konsälobs oles penön söle Ch. in R., kel labom fetanis ko oms, sis yels mödumik.

Spelobs das okanobs binön pöfüdikum oles votikna.

Dünans olsik divodikün,

F. & Ko.

6.

Lemakomit.

Lyon, *mälul* 15*id*, 1887.

*Söle O. Yokohama.*

Begobs oli lemön plo kal obsik e sedön obes ko naf balid kel odevegom al Flentän.
Miglamis 4,000 satina Oshio. No vilobs givön umo ka franis 75 a miglam. If völads satina disoms mödiko, ven ogetol penedi at, valadol-ös vigs kil u fol, bufo lefulol komiti obsik.

Binobs dünans olik divodikün

Ch. & R.

7.

Nunod Lefulama.

Yokohama, *velul* 30*id*, 1887.

*Söles Ch. & e R., Lyon.*

Gepüköl penede olsik de mälul 15*id* yela at, nunob olis das elemob, plo kal e ma komit olsik, miglamis 4,000 Oshiosatina plo frans 70 a miglam.

Segun desid olsik, osedob omis oles ko naf " Le Requin " odevegöl al Marseille, jölul 4*id*.

Opelob obi * me tlat muls kil sis dät.

D. O.

8.

Tlatanunod.

Madrid, *jolul* 25*id*, 1887.

*Söles A. frères, Paris.*

Labob stimi nunön olis atoso das etlatob su ols:
Fr. 2,500 muls 2 sis dät. Noetols-ös tlati obik e lasumol-ös omi gudiko.

D. O.,
H.

---

* *Opelob*, I will pay; *obi*, myself: I will recoup myself.

9.

### Komedapened.

Paris, *balsebalul* 5*id*, 1887.
*Söle H., Wien.*

Pened at polovegivom ole fa söl A. S., bal cifas leböbadoma V. & Ko. in zif obsik.

Söl S. desänom visitön Löstäni al stabön fetanis bevü dom omik e leböbels anik Bömäna e Nugäna.

Labol-ös gudi yufön fleni obik in beginam omik: obinob vemo denik ole plo flenöf keli olabol plok\*m, e kanol numön su dünavil obik, ven flens olik okömoms al Paris.

D. O.,
B.

10.

### Lemakomit.

Stockholm, *balsul* 20*id*, 1886.
*Söles Ch. e F., in Marseille.*

Sukü nunod olsik de 10*id* amula dö stad jäfas in zif olsik, begob olis lemön plo kal obik smatubis 25 leülukaleüla, if tuvols liköfi gudik, suämü fr. 1·80 a miglam.

No lonob tu jalepiko suämi, numöl su ols tefü kud kudadinas obik, ab desidob lefulami fovik komita obik.

Sedols-ös obe lesami smalik, sosus ulemols leüli, e nünols-ös obe otüpo nemis katana e nafa, dat kanob dunön zesüdikosi tefü sefam. If binos mögik, fledols-ös smatubis su naf svedänik.

Kanols cänapenedön su ab plo suäm nota olsik, mul bal sis dät.

Spelob, das obinob ko jäf at balid e das okodom obi denuön oles komitis obik. D. D.,

# APPENDIX I.

## On Euphony.

§ 1. Some Volapükists occasionally place the adjective *before* the noun (see § 6), either to make it emphatic or to avoid a succession of words all ending in *ik* or *lik*; but adjectives which precede the noun are declined and must agree with it. Thus in *Cils binoms gudik*, the adjective remains undeclined; but in *gudiks cils* the adjective agrees with its noun. "The teacher loves good and industrious pupils" may be translated either—*Tidel löfom julelis gudik e dutik;* or, *Tidel löfom gudikis julelis e dutik.*

Similarly it is permissible to use, instead of the possessive pronouns, *obik, olik, omik,* etc., the genitives of the personal pronouns *oba, ola, oma,* etc.; thus instead of *Jiblod olik lejönik*, we may say, *Jiblod ola lejönik.* The same endeavour to avoid the harsh sound *ik* wherever possible has led to the contraction of *mōdiko* into *mōdo, balvotiko* into *balvoto,* and the like.

§ 2. The interrogative particle *li* (§ 8) may follow the verb if euphony requires it; thus we may translate "Do you speak?" either by *li-pükol?* or *pükol-li?*

§ 3. The reflexive pronoun *oki* (§ 17) may be joined to the verb thus:—"They love themselves" may be translated either by (a) *löfoms okis,* or by (b) *löfomsok,* or by (c) *löfokoms.* Translation (a) is no doubt most in harmony with English practice.

---

# APPENDIX II.

## On Groups of Words.*

Roots as a rule consist of two consonants and a vowel between them (§ 5); *e.g.*:—

    *tid,* teach(ing)    *log,* eye    *pük,* speech
    *yag,* chase    *lem,* purchase    *lil,* ear, etc.

They are derived, on certain fixed principles, from Teutonic (English, German, and Dutch) and Latin (French, Italian, and Spanish) words; thus:—

    From the Latin *fuga* is derived *fug,* flight
       ,,      ,,   *caput*   ,,   *kap,* head
       ,,      ,,   *pagus*   ,,   *pag,* village
       ,,      ,,   *populus*   ,,   *pop,* people

---

* For this section the translator is partly indebted to Prof. Pflaumer's *Vollständiger Lehrgang des Volapük.*

From the German *Feld* is derived *fel*, field
„ „ *Bier* „ *bil*, beer
„ „ *Gans* „ *gan*, goose
„ „ *Berg* „ *bel*, mountain
„ English *bring* „ *blin*
„ „ *cloth* „ *klot*
„ „ *skill* „ *skil*
„ „ *time* „ *tim*
„ „ *shore* „ *jol*
„ French *cheval* „ *jeval*, horse
„ „ *quel* „ *kel*, which
„ „ *de nouveau* „ *denu*, anew, again
„ „ *durant* „ *du*, during, etc.

It will be observed that the original words are clipped, that *r* is turned into *l*, and *ng* into *n*. If a word begins with a vowel or an *h* (mute or sounded), the letter *l* is prefixed.

Thus, Latin *oculus* becomes *log*, eye
„ English *ear* „ *lil*
„ French *forêt* „ *fot*, forest
„ Latin *anima* „ *lan*, soul
„ English *ape* „ *lep*
„ French *offre* „ *lof*, offer
„ English *image* „ *mag*; and so on.

From these roots numerous words are formed by composition and by means of prefixes and suffixes.

### EXAMPLES.

*tid*, teach
*tidön*, to teach
*tidel*, teacher
*tidal*, great teacher
*löpatidel*, head-master

*ted*, purchase
*tedön*, to buy
*tedel*, merchant
*tedal*, wholesale merchant

*jut*, shoot
*jutön*, to shoot
*jutel*, he that shoots
*jutal*, marksman

*mat*, matrimony
*matön*, to marry
*matel*, husband
*jimatel*, wife
*matapömetön*, to betroth

*mek*, make
*mekön*, to make
*mekad*, might, power
*mekadik*, powerful, mighty

*jön*, beauty
*jönik*, beautiful
*lejönik*, very beautiful

*buk*, book
*bukil*, little book
*cem*, chamber, room
*cemil*, closet
*bijop*, bishop
*lebijop*, archbishop
*dük*, duke

*ledük*, grand-duke
*duk*, lead
*dukön*, to lead
*nindukön*, to lead in, introduce

*pen*, pen
*penön*, to write

*penel*, writer, clerk
*pened*, a letter
*penäd*, the document
*ninpenäd*, inscription.
*penot*, treatise
*bepenön*, to describe
*disapenön*, to write under, sign
*disapenäd*, signature

*fat*, father
*lufat*, stepfather
*lüfat*, father-in-law

*nim*, animal
*nimav*, zoology
*lanim*, courage
*laniman*, encouragement
*lanimö!* take heart! cheer up!
*lanimälik*, courageous, brave
*lanimäliko*, bravely

*bel*, mountain
*belem*, mountain range
*nebel* (no-mountain), valley

*bled*, leaf
*bledem*, foliage

*log*, eye
*logön*, to see
*denulogön*, to see again
*logad*, vision, sight
*loged*, (a) glance, (a) look

*logod*, face
*lenlog*, view
*lenlogön*, to view, look at
*bülogön*, to foresee (*büfü*)
*logik*, visible
*dulogik*, through-visible, transparent
*loeg*, observation
*loegön*, to observe
*loegöp*, observatory
*logam*, sight, inspection
*zilogam*, circumspection

*pük*, speak
*pukön*, to speak
*pükat*, (a) speech, an address
*pükatön*, to deliver an address
*pükav*, philology
*pükel*, speaker, orator
*püköf*, eloquence
*pükofik*, eloquent
*pükot*, conversation
*okapükot*, soliloquy (*ok*, self)
*telapükot*, dialogue (*tel*, two)
*bepükön*, to speak upon, discuss
*gepükön*, to reply
*lupükön*, to gossip
*nepükön* (not to speak), to be silent
*sepükön*, to speak out, express, pronounce
*tapükön*, to contradict
*depükön*, to dispute

### COMPOUND WORDS.

*pük*, speak
*Flentapük*, the French language
*Volapük*, world-speech
*pükatidel*, teacher of language
*motapük*, mother-tongue
*motazif*, native city
*lit*, light; *pol*, carry
*litapol*, lamp
*lem*, purchase; *cem*, room

*lemacem*, shop
*vöd*, word; *buk*, book
*vödabuk*, dictionary
*mon*, money; *bäled*, age
*bäledamon*, pension
*buk*, book; *tedel*, merchant
*bukatedel*, bookseller
*fil*, fire; *bel*, mountain
*filabel*, volcano

# VOCABULARY.

## VOLAPÜK.

### A AND Ä.

*A*, particle (see p. 29).
*Ä*, prefix (see p. 20).
*Ad*, suffix (see p. 36).
*Af*, suffix (see p. 40).
*Ägüpän*, Egypt.
*Ägüpänel*, Egyptian.
*Al*, suffix (see p. 35).
*Al*, towards.
*Al*, to.
*Alik*, every, each.
*Alos*, thereto.
*Also*, well then.
*Am*, suffix (see p. 35).
*An*, suffix (see p. 39).
*Anik*, any, some, a few.
*Apod*, apple.
*As*, as.
*Äso*, as well as.
*As sam* (see voc. vii.).
*At*, this (person).
*Atna*, this time.
*Atos*, this (thing).
*Atoso*, herewith.
*Av*, suffix (see p. 35).
*Ävendelo*, last evening.
*Ayelo*, last year.

### B.

*Ba* (see voc. iv.).
*Bad*, bad, ill.
*Badik,* } bad, ill (adj.).
*Badlik,*
*Bafō!* bravo!
*Bäk*, back (noun).
*Bakel*, baker.

*Baken*, bakehouse.
*Bakön*, to bake.
*Bal*, one (numeral).
*Bäled*, age.
*Bäledik*, aged, old.
*Bäledan*, a grey-beard, an aged man.
*Bäledanik*, hoary-headed.
*Balid*, the first.
*Balido*, firstly.
*Balion*, a million.
*Balsebalul*, November.
*Balsetelul*, December.
*Balsna*, ten times.
*Balsnalik*, tenth (adj.).
*Balsul*, October.
*Balüdel*, Sunday.
*Balüdo*, at first.
*Balul*, January.
*Balvoto*, each other, mutually, reciprocally.
*Ban*, (a) bath.
*Banön*, to bathe.
*Bayän*, Bavaria.
*Bayanel*, a Bavarian.
*Beatik*, blessed, happy, deceased.
*Bed*, bed.
*Beg*, (a) request.
*Begin*, commencement.
*Beginam*, undertaking, enterprize.
*Beginön*, to begin.
*Begön*, to beg, request.
*Beigolön*, to go by, go past.
*Bel*, mountain.
*Belem*, mountain range.
*Beljän*, Belgium.
*Benik*, good, gracious.

*Beno,* well, good.
*Bepenōn,* to describe.
*Bestimōn,* to honour.
*Bevü,* among.
*Bi,* because.
*Bif,* before (locally).
*Bifo,* in front (locally).
*Bil,* beer, ale.
*Biliet,* ticket.
*Bilōp,* alehouse.
*Bin,* tree.
*Binaklon,* tree top.
*Bin,* being.
*Binōn,* to be.
*Binug,* essence. [pation.
*Biseo,* in advance, in antici-
*Bizugik,* excellent.
*Bizugōn,* to prefer.
*Bläd,* breath.
*Bläg,* blackness.
*Blägik,* black.
*Blefik,* short.
*Blek,* fracture,
*Blekōn,* to break.
*Blibōn,* to remain.
*Blim,* equipment, dowry.
*Blinōn,* to bring.
*Blit,* trowsers.
*Blod,* brother.
*Blöt,* breast.
*Blötaklot,* waistcoat.
*Boad,* wood. [wooden.
*Boadik,* made of wood,
*Bōb,* purse.
*Bod,* bread.
*Böd,* bird.
*Bofik,* both.
*Bömän,* Bohemia.
*Bonedam,* subscription, order.
*Bötel,* waiter, butler. [ally).
*Büf, Büfo,* before (tempor-
*Buk,* book.
*Bukam,* book-keeping.
*Bum,* act of building.
*Bumamasel,* architect.
*Bumot,* (a) building.
*Bumōn,* to build.
*Bün,* (a) pear.
*Büo,* primarily, prelimin-
*But,* boot. [arily.

## C.

*Caf,* kettle. [goods.
*Can,* merchandise, wares,
*Cänapened,* bill of exchange.
*Cänapened balid,* First of ex-
change. [exchange.
*Cänapened telid,* Second of
*Cänapenedōn,* to draw a bill.
*Cedōn,* to think of, to have an
*Cem,* (a) room. [opinion of.
*Cif,* chief, head, principal,
manager.
*Cil,* child.
*Cilän,* Chili.
*Cin,* machine.
*Cinän,* China.
*Cōd,* justice. [bunal.
*Cödef,* court of justice, tri-
*Cödel,* judge.
*Cōdōn,* to judge.

## D.

*Da,* prefix (see p. 36).
*Du,* through.
*Dabalik,* single.
*Dabegōn,* to obtain by asking.
*Daduk,* education.
*Dalam,* authority, power of
attorney, representative
power.
*Dalebōn,* to suffer want, starve.
*Dalitōn,* to light up. [espy.
*Dalogōn,* to catch sight of,
*Dalōn,* to allow, permit.
*Dälōn,* to be allowed.
*Dam,* drama.
*Damatel,* actor.
*Damatelam,* representation.
*Däm,* injury, hurt. [age.
*Dämōn,* to injure, hurt, dam-
*Danemōn,* nominate, appoint.
*Danik,* grateful.
*Danōn,* to thank, owe thanks.
*Danotōn,* to enquire.
*Danü!* thanks!
*Das,* that.
*Dasumōn,* to seize upon, grasp.
*Dat,* in order that.
*Datikōn,* (see *Tikōn*) to invent.

*Datüvön*, to invent, discover.
*Datuv*, invention.
*Datüv*, discovery.
*Davestigön*, to find out by
*De*, of. [searching.
*Deb*, debt.
*Defiledön*, to burn down.
*Deil*, death.
*Deilön*, to die.
*Deköm*, descent, derivation.
*Del*, suffix (see p. 34).
*Del*, day.
*Delid*, dearth. [costly.
*Delidik*, dear, expensive,
*Delo*, by day.
*Demü*, on account of.
*Deno*, nevertheless.
*Denu*, again, anew.
*Denuön*, to repeat.
*Des*, from . . . till.
*Desän*, design, intention.
*Desäno*, intentionally, designedly.
*Desänön*, to intend, plan.
*Desedön*, to send away.
*Desid*, desire.
*Det*, right hand.
*Detük*, right (not left).
*Deutän*, Germany.
*Deutel*, (a) German.
*Deutik*, German (adj.).
*Devegön*, to depart, leave harbour.
*Devod*, devotion, worship.
*Devodik*, devotional.
*Di*, prefix (see p. 40).
*Dibatonön*, to growl.
*Diblekön*, to break in pieces, shiver, shatter.
*Dido*, indeed, certainly.
*Difik*, different, various.[melt.
*Diflumön*, to flow asunder,
*Dil*, (a) part.
*Dilo*, partly.
*Dimidön*, to rend, tear.
*Din*, thing.
*Dis*, under.
*Disapenäd*, signature.
*Disik*, the lower.
*Diso*, below, at foot.

*Disön*, to go down, to set, to sink.
*Distukön*, to pull down, destroy.
*Divodik*, devoted.
*Dled*, fear, dread.
*Dledön*, to dread, fear.
*Dleföl*, hitting the mark, fit, suitable, appropriate.
*Dlefön*, to hit.
*Dlen*, (a) tear.
*Dlenön*, to weep.
*Dlin*, (a) beverage.
*Dlinön*, to drink.
*Do*, although.
*Dö*, of, concerning.
*Dog*, dog.
*Dök*, duck.
*Dol*, pain.
*Dom*, house.
*Domem*, house gear.
*Domem taimik*, earthenware,
*Domo*, at home. [crockery,
*Du*, whilst.
*Dub*, by means of.
*Dugön*, to lead.
*Dük*, duke.
*Dukön*, to lead, carry.
*Dul*, duration.
*Dulöf*, durability.
*Dulön*, to last, endure.
*Dunan*, agent.
*Dunanät*, agency.
*Dünal*, servant (of higher rank), minister.
*Dunavil*, willingness to serve (cf. vilön).
*Dünel*, servant (of lower rank), boots, porter.
*Dunik*, active.
*Dunön*, to do, act, practice.
*Dünön*, to serve.
*Dunön*, to do.
*Düp*, hour.
*Dut*, industry.
*Dutik*, industrious.

E

*E*, and.
*E* . . . *e*, as well as.
*Ed*, suffix (see p. 35).

*Ef*, suffix (see p. 36).
*Egelo*, always.
*Ek*, somebody.
*Eko*, behold, here (Lat. *ecce*).
*El*, suffix (see p. 26).
*Em*, suffix (see p. 40).
*En*, suffix (see p. 40).
*Et*, that (person).
*Etos*, that (thing).
*Evelo*, ever, at any time.

## F

*Fa*, of, from, by, by means of, on the part of.
*Fag*, distance.
*Fagik*, far, distant.
*Fälo*, further, in future.
*Falön*, to fall.
*Fälön*, to fell.
*Fat*, father.
*Fatän*, fatherland.
*Fatänäl*, patriotism.
*Fatel*, grandfather.
*Fäd*, chance.
*Fädiko*, by chance, haply.
*Fe*, prefix (see p. 36).
*Fe*, in truth, in faith, truly.
*Fedugön*, to mislead, seduce.
*Fegebön*, to use up, consume.
*Fegolön*, to pass away, elapse, [perish.
*Feil*, acre.
*Feilel*, peasant.
*Feilem* and *feilöm*, agricultural implements.
*Fetan*, relationship, connection.
*Fiam*, commercial firm.
*Fidön*, to eat, dine.
*Fikop*, Africa.
*Fikopel*, (an) African.
*Fikulik*, difficult.
*Fil*, fire.
*Filabel*, volcano.
*Filed*, conflagration.
*Filedön*, to burn.
*Filosop*, philosophy.
*Fimän*, (a) continent, large mass of land.
*Fin*, end.
*Finam*, termination.

*Fined*, finger.
*Fino*, finally.
*Fit*, fish.
*Fizir*, officer.
*Flap*, a blow.
*Flapön*, to strike.
*Fled*, load, cargo, freight.
*Flekolön*, to turn.
*Flen*, friend.
*Flenöf*, friendliness.
*Flent*, *Flentän*, France.
*Flentel*, (a) Frenchman.
*Flentik*, French (adj.).
*Flenüg*, friendship.
*Flif*, freshness.
*Flifik*, fresh.
*Flit*, flight.
*Flodön*, to freeze.
*Flol*, flower.
*Flolatim*, spring.
*Fluk*, fruit.
*Flukatim*, autumn.
*Flum*, river.
*Flumön*, to flow.
*Fö*, prefix (see p. 36).
*Foginel*, foreigner.
*Fögivön*, to forgive.
*Fol*, four.
*Foldil*, a quarter part.
*Folul*, April.
*Folüdel*, Wednesday.
*Fömad*, cheese.
*Fösefön*, to assure, asseverate.
*Fot*, forest.
*Foviko*, forthwith, immediately, anon.
*Foxaf*, fox.
*Fug*, flight.
*Fulön*, to fill.
*Fümik*, sure, precise, reliable.
*Fun*, corpse.
*Fün*, foundation.
*Funön*, to kill.
*Fünön*, to found, establish.
*Fünam*, the founding, establishing.
*Füsüd*, physics.
*Fut*, foot.
*Futaveged*, footsteps.
*Futo*, on foot.

*Futel*, pedestrian.
*Futelön*, to walk.

## G

*Ga*, still, however, but.
*Gab*, earl, count.
*Gad*, garden.
*Gadel*, gardener.
*Gadem*, garden tools.
*Gäl*, joy.
*Gälod*, pleasure.
*Gälön*, to gladden.
*Ge*, prefix (see p. 40).
*Gebön*, to use.
*Gedlanön*, to push back.
*Geil*, height, summit.
*Geilik*, high.
*Gepük*, (a) reply.
*Gesagön*, to reply.
*Getön*, to get.
*Gevegön*, to travel back.
*Git*, right (Lat. *jus*).
*Gitav*, jurisprudence.
*Givön*, to give.
*Glad*, ice.
*Gladajuk*, (a) skate.
*Gladajukön*, to skate.
*Glam*, gram.
*Glät*, glass, tumbler.
*Glätik*, made of glass.
*Glebelem*, chief mountain range.
*Gleflen*, intimate friend.
*Glet*, magnitude.
*Gletam*, increase, expansion, enlargement.
*Gletav*, mathematics.
*Gletik*, large, big, great.
*Glezif*, chief town, capital.
*Glik*, Greece.
*Glikel*, (a) Greek.
*Glüg*, church.
*Glum*, gloom.
*Glün*, green.
*Glüned*, vegetables.
*God*, God.
*Godav*, theology.
*Godavel*, theologian.
*Golön*, to go.
*Golüd*, gold.

*Gödel*, morning.
*Gödelo*, in the morning.
*Gud*, goodness.
*Gudik*, good.
*Gudikel*, the good man.
*Gued*, estate.
*Gün*, gun.
*Gutön*, to taste.
*Günapur*, gunpowder.

## H

*Hät*, hat.
*Hel*, hair.
*Het*, hatred.
*Hetlik*, ugly.
*Hit*, heat.
*Hitatim*, summer.

## I

*I*, also.
*Ibo*, because.
*Id*, suffix (see p. 26).
*If*, if, when.
*Ik*, suffix (see p. 14).
*In*, in.
*Ino*, inside.
*Is*, here.
*Isik*, of this place.
*It* (see voc. iv.).

## J

*Jäf*, business affairs.
*Jalepik*, strict, rigid, rigorous.
*Jedön*, to throw, cast.
*Jekön*, to startle, scare.
*Jem*, shame.
*Jemod*, disgrace.
*Jeval*, horse.
*Jevalel*, horseman, horse-soldier.
*Ji*, fem. prefix.
*Jidünel*, maidservant.
*Jikösel*, cousin (f.).
*Jinön*, to shine, seem, appear.
*Jipul*, girl.
*Jlesän*, Silesia.
*Jol*, shore, coast.
*Jöl*, eight.
*Jölul*, August (the month).
*Jön*, beauty.

*Jönik*, beautiful.
*Jotlän*, Scotland.
*Jueg*, sugar.
*Juitön*, to enjoy.
*Juk*, shoe.
*Jul*, school.
*Julabuk*, school-book.
*Julel*, scholar, pupil.
*Jü*, till.
*Jünu*, hitherto.
*Jutön*, to shoot.
*Jveiz*, *Jveizän*, Switzerland.
*Jveizel*, a Swiss.

## K.

*Ka*, than.
*Kaf*, coffee.
*Kal*, calculation, account.
*Kaled*, calendar, almanac.
*Kalod*, cold (noun).
*Kalodik*, cold (adj.).
*Kalön*, to calculate.
*Kanitön*, to sing.
*Kanitel*, singer, minstrel.
*Kanön* (see voc. vi.).
*Kap*, head.
*Kapäl*, intelligence.
*Kapälik*, intelligent.
*Kapälön*, to understand.
*Kapälüb*, intelligence.
*Käf*, stratagem, trick.
*Käfik*, sly.
*Kän*, cannon.
*Kat*, cat.
*Katan*, captain.
*Kaut*, caution.
*Kautik*, cautious.
*Kautiko*, cautiously.
*Kel*, which (person).
*Kelos*, which (thing). }(rel.)
*Kiem*, chemistry.
*Kif* (see voc. iv.).
*Kikod*, for what cause, wherefore, why.
*Kil*, three.
*Kilel*, a triplet.
*Kilid*, the third.
*Kilido*, thirdly.
*Kilön*, to treble.

*Kilul*, March (the month)
*Kilüdel*, Tuesday.
*Kim* (see voc. iv.).
*Kimid?* the how manieth?
*Kinän*, kingdom, empire.
*Kitön*, to give quittance, sign receipt.
*Kiof* (see voc. iv.).
*Kiom* (see voc. iv.).
*Kiöp?* where?
*Kios* (see voc. iv.).
*Kiplad?* where?
*Kiplada?* whence?
*Kipladi?* whither?
*Kis* (see voc. iv.).
*Kiüp?* when? at what time?
*Kleilik*, loud, clear.
*Klig*, war.
*Klöd*, belief.
*Klödat*, credit.
*Klödön*, to believe.
*Klöf*, cloth.
*Klon*, top.
*Klot*, garment.
*Klülik*, clear.
*Ko*, with, together with.
*Kö*, where (relative).
*Kod*, cause.
*Kodo*, on which account, for which cause.
*Kodön*, to cause.
*Komed*, recommendation.
*Komip*, (a) combat.
*Komipel*, combatant.
*Komipön*, to combat.
*Komit*, commission, order.
*Kömön*, to come.
*Kön*, narrative.
*Konfidön*, to trust, entrust.
*Konön*, to narrate.
*Konsälön*, to advise.
*Konsidön*, to consider, regard.
*Konzed*, concert.
*Kösefön*, to sacrifice.
*Kosek*, consecration-festival.
*Kösekön*, to sacrifice, devote.
*Kösel*, cousin (m.).
*Kösemo*, habitually.
*Koskömön*, to come to meet, to meet.

*Kösömön*, to be wont (Lat. *solere*).
*Kostön*, to cost.
*Kotenik*, satisfied, pleased.
*Krit*, Christ.
*Kritav*, Christianity.
*Kritef*, Christendom.
*Kritik*, Christian (adj.).
*Kud*, care.
*Kudadin*, concern, affair.
*Kuk*, kitchen.
*Kukaneif*, kitchen-knife.
*Kukel*, a cook.
*Kukön*, to cook.

## L

*La*, suffix (see p. 28).
*Lä*, at the (Fr. *chez*).
*Läb*, fortune, luck.
*Labed*, possession.
*Labem*, property, wealth.
*Lābik*, lucky, fortunate.
*Lābo*, luckily.
*Labön*, to have.
*Lād*, lady.
*Lad*, heart.
*Ladälod*, mood.
*Ladlik*, heartily, cordially.
*Laf*, half (noun, Fr. *moitié*).
*Lafayel*, half year.
*Lain*, wool.
*Lak*, lake.
*Lanimälik*, bravely.
*Län*, land, country.
*Lapin*, prey, booty.
*Lapinön*, to rob.
*Lapinel*, robber.
*Lasumon*, to take up (cf. *suniön*).
*Lat*, late.
*Lätik*, last.
*Le*, magnifying prefix (see p. 18).
*Lebalik*, unique.
*Lebeno*, very good.
*Leblimön*, to establish.
*Lebōb*, bank (cf. *bōb*).
*Ledik*, red.
*Ledom*, palace.
*Ledük*, grand-duke.

*Ledükān*, duchy.
*Lefulam*, the carrying out, execution.
*Lefulön*, to fulfil, to carry out.
*Lefüd*, east, orient.
*Legivot*, (a) present, gift.
*Lehät*, helmet.
*Leigūpo*, at the same time.
*Leil*, mile.
*Lein*, lion.
*Leitik*, light (not heavy).
*Lejönik*, exceedingly beautiful.
*Lek*, echo.
*Lekanitel*, master-singer.
*Lel*, iron.
*Lelod*, railway.
*Lem*, (a) purchase.
*Lemacem*, shop.
*Lemän*, remainder.
*Lemasel*, great master.
*Lemōn*, to buy.
*Len*, at, by.
*Lenadön*, to learn.
*Lenlilön*, to listen to.
*Leno*, not at all.
*Lensumön*, to accept.
*Lenu*, immediately.
*Lep*, ape, monkey.
*Lesagön*, to assure.
*Lesam*, pattern, sample.
*Lesumik*, agreeable.
*Leül*, oil.
*Leüluk*, olive.
*Letön*, to let.
*Leyan*, gate.
*Li*, prefix (see p. 17).
*Liān*, verse.
*Lib*, liberty.
*Libik*, free, open.
*Libōn*, to liberate, set free.
*Liedō*, unfortunately.
*Lieg*, riches.
*Liegik*, rich, wealthy.
*Liev*, hare.
*Lif*, life.
*Lifön*, to live.
*Lifüp*, a lifetime.
*Liko?* how?
*Likōf*, constitution, nature of thing, quality.

*Lil*, ear.
*Liladön*, to read.
*Lilön*, to hear.
*Limödik?* how much?
*Lip*, lip.
*Litön*, to give light, shine.
*Lob*, praise.
*Lobön*, to praise.
*Lodam*, load, cargo.
*Lodön*, to load.
*Lödön*, to dwell, inhabit.
*Loet*, roast meat.
*Löfan*, lover.
*Löfik*, loved, dear.
*Löfön*, to love.
*Logön*, to see.
*Lölik*, whole.
*Lömibön*, to rain.
*Loned*, length.
*Lonedön*, to lengthen.
*Lonün*, to fix, determine.
*Lönön*, to belong.
*Lop*, opera.
*Löpik*, the upper.
*Löpo*, above, upstairs.
*Löpöf*, superior authority.
*Löstän*, Austria.
*Lot*, guest.
*Lotöp*, *Lotug*, inn, hotel, hostelry.
*Lovegivön*, to hand over, deliver.
*Lovemelik*, beyond the sea, transoceanic.
*Lovik*, gently, softly.
*Lovopükön*, to speak softly, whisper.
*Lu*, diminutive prefix (see p. 17).
*Ludog*, wolf.
*Ludom*, hut.
*Lufat*, stepfather.
*Lufidön* (see *Fidön*).
*Lüg*, sorrow.
*Lügapled*, tragedy.
*Lugivön*, to lend.
*Luhät*, cap.
*Luimön*, to moisten, wet.

*Lukijafön*, to procure.
*Lukilogam*, view, prospect.
*Lul*, five.
*Luladäl*, sadness, melancholy.
*Lulel*, a fiver.
*Lulön*, to quintuple.
*Lulul*, May (the month).
*Lulüdel*, Thursday.
*Lupab*, caterpillar.
*Lusän*, Russia.
*Lusänel*, (a) Russian.
*Lusänik*, Russian (adj.).
*Lut*, air.
*Lutik*, airy.
*Luüno*, at least.
*Luvokön*, to cry aloud (cf. *vokön*).
*Luvomik*, womanish.

## M.

*Ma*, conformably, in accordance with.
*Mad*, maturity.
*Madik*, ripe, mature.
*Mafōf*, moderation. [=1*s*.
*Mak*, (a) mark, German coin
\**Makab*, (a) famous thing.
*Mäkab*, fame.
*Mäkabik*, famous, celebrated.
*Mäl*, six.
*Malädik*, ill.
*Malädikel*, (a) patient.
*Malädön*, to fall ill.
*Malön*, to announce, indicate.
*Mälüdel*, Friday.
*Mälul*, June.
*Man*, man (Lat. *vir*).
*Masel*, master.
*Mat* and *Mated*, marriage, matrimony.
*Matel*, husband.
*Matapömetön*, to betroth.
*Mayed*, majesty.
*Me*, with, by means of.
*Med*, middle.
*Medam*, action of intermediary.

---

\* *Makabs sifa*, wonders, sights of a city.

*Medin*, medicine. [cine.
*Medinav*, the science of medi-
*Medinel*, physician, surgeon.
*Meditön*, to meditate, consider, think.
*Medön*, to act as intermediary (cf. *med.*).
*Meinöp*, a mine.
*Mekad*, might, power.
*Mekadik*, mighty.
*Mekön*, to make.
*Me*, with, by means of.
*Mel*, the sea, ocean.
*Melak*, intercourse.
*Melop*, America.
*Melopel*, (an) American.
*Men*, man (Lat. *homo*).
*Menad*, humanity, mankind.
*Met*, metre (39·37 in.),
*\*Miglam*, kilogram.
*Migön*, to mix, mingle.
*Mil*, a thousand.
*Milagön*, to admire.
*Mileg*, butter.
*Milig*, milk.
*Milmet*, kilometre = 5 furlongs.
*Min*, mineral.
*Minav*, mineralogy.
*Mit*, meat, flesh.
*Mödik*, much.
*Mödiks*, many.
*Mödo*, much (see p. 21).
*Mögik*, possible.
*Mogonön*, to run away, escape.
*Mon*, money.
*Monamed*, monetary means (cf. *med*).
*Monitel*, (a) rider. [mal].
*Monitön*, to ride (on an ani-
*Mot*, mother. [*Tävön*.
*Motävön*, to start from (see
*Motöf*, birth.
*Motöfazif*, native town.
*Motöfik*, native of.
*Mucuk*, mule.
*Mufön*, to move.
*Mul*, month.
*Mun*, moon.

*Musig*, music.
*Musigel*, musician.
*Mütön* (see voc. vi.).

## N.

*Na*, suffix (see p. 27)
*Nad*, needle.
*Naf*, ship.
*Nakömön*, to arrive.
*Nam*, hand.
*Näm*, strength, power.
*Nämik*, strong, vigorous.
*Nämön*, to invigorate,
*Nat*, nature. [strengthen.
*Natav*, natural science.
*Ne*, prefix (see p. 23).
*Neb*, near by.
*Nebel*, valley.
*Nedet*, left, not right (cf. *det*).
*Nedön*, to need, want.
*Nef*, nephew.
*Nefikulik*, easy.
*Neflen*, enemy.
*Negelo*, never.
*Neif*, knife.
*Neit*, night.
*Neito*, at night.
*Nejemik*, shameless.
*Nek*, nobody.
*Neläbo*, unluckily.
*Nelabön*, to lack.
*Nelijän*, England.
*Nelijel*, Englishman.
*Nelijik*, English (adj.).
*Neluimön*, to wipe, dry.
*Nelüm*, thirst.
*Nem*, name.
*Nemödik*, few.
*Nemön*, to name.
*Nen*, without (Lat. *sine*).
*Nendas*, without that, unless.
*Nepöko*, free from fault (cf. *pök.*).
*Nepük*, silence.
*Nevelo*, never.
*Ni . . . ni*, neither . . . nor.
*Nidän*, India.
*Nif*, snow.

---

\* *Mi*, contr. from *mil* = 1,000; cf. *glam*.

*Nifatim*, winter.
*Nifön*, to snow.
*Nik*, suffix (see p. 29).
*Nil*, vicinity, neighbourhood.
*Nilel*, neighbour.
*Nilik*, near.
*Nilön*, to approach.
*Nilü*, near by.
*Nim*, animal.
*Nimav*, zoology.
*Ninflumön*, to terminate (said of a river), to flow into.
*Ninavag*, cave.
*Nindilam*, classification, grouping, distribution.
*Nindilön*, to classify, group, distribute.
*Ninlödel*, inhabitant.
*Nitlidön*, to enter.
*Niver*, university.
*No nog*, not yet.
*Nö*, not very.
*Noetön*, to take note of, notice.
*Nog*, as yet.
*Nök*, uncle.
*Nol*, knowledge.
*Nolel*, scholar, savant.
*Nolik*, scientific.
*Nolön*, to know.
*Nolüd*, north.
*Nolümelop*, North America.
*Nolümelopel*, (a) North American.
*Nonik*, no, none (adverbially).
*Nos*, nothing.
*Not*, information, announcement.
*Nu*, now.
*Nud*, nose.
*Nugän*, Hungary.
*Nulik*, new.
*Nulüd*, food, nourishment.
*Num*, number.
*Numōn*, to count.
*Nün*, information, communication.
*Nunod*, report, communication.
*Nunön*, to announce.

## O AND Ö.

*O*, prefix (see p. 20).
*O*, suffix (see pp. 26, 35).
*Ö! ahi! eh!*
*Ö*, suffix (see p. 40).
*Ob*, I.
*Obik*, my.
*Öd*, suffix (see p. 26).
*Odelo*, to-morrow.
*Of*, she.
*Of*, suffix (see p. 40).
*Ofen*, often. [fem. noun].
*Ofik*, his or her (before a
*Ok*, himself, herself, itself.
*Ol*, suffix (see p. 31).
*Olik*, thy. [masc. noun].
*Omik*, his or her (before a
*Ön*, suffix (see p. 26).
*Op*, suffix (see p. 39).
*Op*, suffix (see p. 39).
*Os*, suffix (see p. 26).
*Ot*, the same.
*Otüpo*, at the same time, contemporaneously (cf. *tüp*).
*Öv*, suffix (see p. 29).
*Ovi*, over.

## P.

*Pab*, butterfly.
*Paels*, parents.
*Pag*, village.
*Pakön*, to spread.
*Panemön*, to be called, named.
*Pato*, specially.
*Paun*, lb. (also £).
*Pein*, pine-tree.
*Pejeköl*, startled.
*Pelam*, payment.
*Pelön*, to pay.
*Pened*, (a) letter (Lat. *epistola*).
*Penön*, to write.
*Pesetenöl*, extensive.
*Pesevo* (see voc. x.).
*Pir*, pyramid.
*Plä*, except.
*Pladön*, to place. [aware of.
*Plakön*, to learn, become
*Plan*, plant.

E

*Planav,* botany.
*Pled,* piece, play.
*Pledön,* to play.
*Plidön,* to please.
*Pliem,* house gear.
*Plin,* prince.
*Plo,* for.
*Plobo,* properly, thoroughly.
*Plofed,* professor.
*Plökön,* to pluck.
*Plös,* therefor, for it.
*Plu ka,* more than.
*Poed,* poetry, poesy.
*Poedal,* (a) great poet.
*Poedat,* poem.
*Poedel,* poet.
*Pof,* haven, port.
*Pöf,* poverty.
*Pöfik,* poor.
*Pöfüd,* profit.
*Pöfüdik,* profitable, useful.
*Pök,* fault.
*Pökik,* faulty.
*Pölig,* danger.
*Pöligik,* dangerous.
*Polön,* to carry.
*Pom,* fruit (Lat. *pomum*).
*Pömetön,* to promise, engage.
*Pon,* bridge.
*Pön,* penalty.
*Pöp,* paper.
*Pöpem,* copybook (Fr. *cahier*).
*Por,* portion.
*Pos,* after.
*Postab,* desert (cf. *tab*).
*Pötit,* appetite.
*Püd,* peace.
*Pük, Pükad,* speech.
*Pükav,* philology.
*Pükön,* to speak.
*Pükot,* conversation, dialogue.
*Pul,* boy.
*Pur,* powder.

+ also pükat

R.

*Reg,* king.
*Rivön,* to reach, attain.
*Romel,* (a) Roman.

S.

*Sagön,* to say.
*Sak,* (a) sack.
*Säkön,* to ask.
*Sanel,* physician, surgeon.
*Sap,* wisdom.
*Sapal,* sage.
*Sapav,* philosophy.
*Satin,* silk.
*Sätön,* to suffice, be enough.
*Saun,* health.
*Saunik,* healthy.
*Saxän,* Saxony.
*Se,* out, out of.
*Sedön,* to send.
*Sefam,* insurance.
*Sefik,* secure, safe.
*Sefön,* to secure, insure, make safe.
*Segun,* according.
*Seilön,* to be silent, to keep secret.
*Seistön,* to lie, be situated.
*Seledik,* seldom.
*Sembal,* some one, a certain one.
*Senilön,* to perceive, feel.
*Senön,* to feel.
*Seslupön,* to slip out.
*Setenön,* to extend, stretch.
*Sevokön,* to exclaim.
*Sevön,* to know (Fr. *connaître*).
*Si,* yes.
*Siadön,* to set.
*Sibinön,* to exist (Fr. *se trouver*).
*Sikik,* distinguished.
*Sikod,* therefore.
*Sil,* the sky, firmament.
*Silop,* Asia.
*Silopel,* Asiatic.
*Simulön,* to simulate, pretend.
*Sis,* since.
*Skanön,* to vex.
*Skit,* leather.
*Slifön,* to slip, fall.
*Slip,* sleep.
*Slipön,* to sleep.
*Slup,* slip. [shelter.
*Slupöp,* loophole, hiding-place,

*Sma*, dimin. prefix (see p. 18).
*Smabed*, nest.
*Smabim*, shrub.
*Smacem*, small room, boudoir.
*Smalik*, small.
*Smalöf*, trifle.
*Smazigad*, cigarette.
*Smilön*, to smile, laugh.
*Smokön*, to smoke.
*Snek*, snake.
*Snekofit*, eel.
*So*, so.
*Sog*, company.
*Sol*, the sun.
*Söl*, master, Mr., sir.
*Solat*, soldier.
*Som*, such.
*Son*, son.
*Sosus*, as soon as.
*Sotimo*, at times, occasionally. [nomical.
*Spälik*, sparing, thrifty, economical.
*Spälön*, to put by, economise.
*Spartän*, Sparta (country).
*Spartänel*, (a) Spartan.
*Spän*, Spain.
*Spat*, (a) walk.
*Spatön*, to take a walk.
*Spel*, hope (noun).
*Spid*, speed.
*Spidö!* be quick! quickly!
*Spidön*, to hasten.
*Spod*, correspondence.
*Spodön*, to correspond.
*Spog*, sponge.
*Stab*, foundation, bottom.
*Stabiko*, from the bottom, thoroughly.
*Stabön*, to establish.
*Stad*, state, position.
*Stadön* (see voc. iv.).
*Stäg*, stag.
*Stan*, stand.
*Stanöf*, constancy.
*Staud*, dining-room, restaurant.
*Stebön*, to stay, tarry.
*Stem*, steam.
*Stepön*, to step, stride, wade.
*Stib*, pencil.

*Stigön*, to urge, induce.
*Stil*, silent.
*Stim*, honour.
*Stimön*, to honour.
*Stit*, establishment.
*Stof*, stuff, material.
*Stök*, storey, floor (of a house).
*Stopön*, to stop.
*Stom*, weather.
*Ston*, a stone.
*Studel*, a student.
*Studön*, to study.
*Stuk*, edifice, structure.
*Stun*, astonishment.
*Stunik*, astonishing.
*Stunön*, to be astonished.
*Su*, up, upon, on.
*Suäm*, price, sum.
*Suämön*, to amount.
*Suemön*, to comprehend.
*Süenön*, to hesitate.
*Suflagön*, to summon, challenge.
*Sufön*, to suffer.
*Sugiv*, task, exercise.
*Sukön*, to follow.
*Sükön*, to seek.
*Sukü*, following, in accordance with.
*Sulogön*, to inspect, survey.
*Sulüd*, south.
*Sumön*, to take.
*Süm*, similarity, analogy.
*Sümik*, similar, analogous.
*Suno*, soon.
*Sup*, soup.
*Süpitön*, to surprise, overtake, befall.
*Suseitön*, to load.
*Sustanön*, to get up, rise.
*Süt*, street, road.

ولَه  تِش  وَم T:

*Tab*, table.
*Tabak*, tobacco.
*Taben*, carpenter's shop.
*Taim*, clay.
*Taimik*, made of clay, earthen.
*Tak*, rest.

*Taked*, repose.
*Takedön*, to repose.
*Tal*, earth.
*Täl*, *Tälän*, Italy.
*Talav*, geology.
*Taled*, geography.
*Talop*, Australia.
*T'alopel*, Australian.
*Tän*, then.
*Tasteifam*, resistance, defence.
*Täv*, journey, voyage.
*Tävel*, traveller.
*Tävön*, to travel.
*Te*, only, not till.
*Teat*, theatre, stage.
*Ted*, trade, commerce.
*Tedadom*, commercial house.
*Tedal*, wholesale merchant.
*Tedel*, merchant, trader.
*Tedön*, to trade.
*Tefü*, concerning, respecting.
*Tel*, two.
*Teldik*, many a one.
*Telel*, (a) pair.
*Telid*, the second.
*Telido*, secondly.
*Telön*, to double.
*Telsidna*, the twentieth time.
*Telsidno*, for the twentieth time.
*Telsnalik*, twentieth (adj.).
*Telüdel*, Monday.
*Telul*, February.
*Tenalik*, eternal.
*Ti*, almost.
*Tid*, act of teaching, lesson, instruction.
*Tidel*, teacher.
*Tidön*, to teach.
*Tied*, tea.
*Tif*, thief, theft.
*Tik*, thought.
*Tikäl*, spirit.
*Tikam*, consideration.
*Tikav*, logic.
*Tikön*, to think.
*Tim*, time.
*Timil*, moment.
*Timilo*, momentarily.
*Tlat*, draft, bill of exchange.

*Tlep*, fright, terror.
*Tlidön*, to tread, step.
*To*, in spite of.
*Töbo*, hardly.
*Tolad*, custom, import or export duty.
*Toladal*, custom-house officer.
*Toladön*, to pay toll or duty.
*Ton*, (a) tone.
*Toned*, (a) ton (1,000 kilogs.).
*Tonod*, loud sound.
*Topöf*, region, landscape.
*Töt*, thunder (noun).
*Tötön*, to thunder.
*Tu*, to, too.
*Tudunön*, to exaggerate.
*Tugedik*, together, in common, common.
*Tuig*, twig, branch.
*Tulön*, to turn.
*Tum*, hundred.
*Tupön*, to disturb.
*Tüp*, period of time.
*Tuvemaf*, monster.
*Tuvön*, to find.
*Türän*, Thuringia.

## U AND Ü.

*U*, or.
*Ü*, suffix (see p. 40).
*Ud*, suffix (see p. 39).
*Udelo*, the day after to-morrow.
*Ug*, suffix (see p. 40).
*Ul*, suffix (see p. 34).
*Umo*, more, in a higher degree.
*Up*, suffix (see p. 40).
*Us*, there.
*Usik*, of that place.
*Ut*, he (dem. pron.).

## V.

*Va*, if, whether.
*Vab*, wagon, cart, carriage.
*Vadelo*, daily, every day.
*Vag*, vacuum.
*Valadön*, to wait.

*Valadöp*, waiting room.
*Valemo*, generally.
*Valik*, all.
*Valiko*, in general.
*Valikodik*, universal. [where.
*Valöpo*, ⸚ universally, every-
*Vam*, warmth.
*Vamik*, warm.
*Vanlik*, in vain.
*Vanliko*, vainly.
*Vat*, water.
*Ved*, origin.
*Vedön*, to become.
*Veg*, way, road.
*Vegön*, to travel.
*Vekömö!* welcome!
*Vel*, seven.
*Velat*, truth.
*Velatik*, true.
*Velatön*, to speak the truth.
*Velul*, July.
*Velüdel*, Saturday.
*Vemo*, very.
*Ven*, when.
*Vendel*, evening.
*Venud*, charm, beauty.
*Vestigön*, to investigate.
*Vesüd*, west.
*Vetik*, weighty, heavy.
*Veütik*, weighty, important.
*Vid*, width, latitude.
*Vig*, week.
*Vikod*, victory.
*Vikodön*, to conquer.
*Viliko*, willingly.
*Vilön*, to will.
*Vip*, (a) wish.
*Vipön*, to wish.
*Vin*, wine.
*Visit*, (a) visit.
*Visitön*, to visit.
*Vo*, true, truly.
*Vob*, work.
*Vobel*, worker, workman.
*Vobön*, to work.
*Vöbön*, to acquire.
*Vokön*, to cry.
*Vol*, world.
*Volapük*, world-speech, universal language.

*Völad*, worth, value, price.
*Vom*, woman.
*Vomik*, womanly.
*Vomül*, Miss.
*Votik*, other.
*Vöd*, word.
*Völ*, wall.
*Vüno*, once upon a time, formerly.
*Votikna*, another time.
*Vun* (a) wound.
*Vunön*, to wound.

## W.

*Wien*, Vienna.

## X.

*Xab*, axis, axle.

## Y.

*Ya*, already.
*Yag*, chase, hunt.
*Yagel*, huntsman.
*Yagön*, to hunt.
*Yan*, door.
*Yed*, but, however.
*Yel*, year.
*Yelatim*, season.
*Yelatum*, century.
*Yof*, delight, merriment.
*Yofapled*, comedy.
*Yuf*, help.
*Yufön*, to help.
*Yulop*, Europe.
*Yulopel*, (a) European.
*Yun*, youth (Lat. *juventa*).
*Yunel*, (a) youth, young man.
*Yunik*, young.
*Yunlik*, youthful.

## Z.

*Zab*, oats.
*Zeil*, goal.
*Zel*, festivity.
*Zeläl*, festive mood.
*Zelik*, festive, solemn.
*Zendel*, midday.
*Zeneit*, midnight.
*Zenodü*, in the middle.

*Zepam,* consent, approval, certificate.
*Zepön,* to consent, approve.
*Zesüdik,* necessary, needful.
*Zesüdön,* to be necessary.
*Zib,* food.
*Zif,* town, city.
*Zigad,* cigar.
*Zil,* zeal.
*Zilik,* zealous.
*Zit,* case, occurrence.

*Zü,* round, around.
*Zül,* nine.
*Zülag,* (a) circular.
*Zülul,* September.
*Züm,* circle.
*Zümön,* to encircle, surround.
*Zümöp,* environs.
*Zun,* anger.
*Zunik,* angry.
*Züp,* appendix.
*Züpel,* adherent, follower, dis- [ciple.

# VOCABULARY.

## ENGLISH.

### A.

Above, *upstairs*, löpo.
According, segun.
Account, *calculation*, kal.
Acquire (verb), vöbön.
Acre, *field*, feil.
Act of teaching, *lesson, instruction*, tid.
Active, dunik.
Actor, damatel.
Adherent, *follower, disciple*, züpel.
Admire, milagön.
Advise, konsälön.
Africa, Fikop.
African (noun), Fikopel.
After, pos.
Again, denu.
Age, bäled.
Aged, bäledik.
Aged man, bäledan.
Agent, dunan.
Agreeable, lesumik.
Agricultural *implements*, feilem, feilöm.
Air, lut.
Airy, lutik.
Ale, *beer*, bil.
Alehouse, bilöp.
All, valik.
Allow, dalön.
Almost, ti.
Already, ya.
Also, i.
Although, do.
Always, egelo.
America, Melop.
American (noun), Melopel.

Amidst, zenodü.
Among, bevü.
Amount (verb), suämön.
Anger, zun.
Angry, zunik.
Animal, nim.
Announce, *indicate*, malön.
And, e.
Any, anïk.
Ape, *monkey*, lep.
Appear, *seem, shine*, jinön.
Appendix, züp.
Appetite, pötit.
Apple, apod.
Approach, nilön.
Appropriate, *fit, suitable*, dleföl.
April, Folul.
Architect, bumamasel.
Arrive, nakömön.
As, as.
As yet, nog.
Asia, Silop.
Asiatic (noun), Silopel.
Ask (verb), säkön.
Assure, *asseverate*, föseföa.
As soon as, sosus.
As well as, äso.
Astonished, to be, stunön.
Astonishing, stunik.
Astonishment, stun.
At, *by*, len.
Attain, *reach*, rivön.
At home, domo.
At least, lutlno.
At times, *occasionally*, sotimo.
August, Jöhul.
Australia, Talop.

*Australian* (noun), Talopel.
*Author*, bukel.
*Autumn*, flukatim.
*Axis, axle*, xab.

### B.

*Back* (noun), bäk.
*Bad* (adj.), bad.
*Bad* (adv.), badik, badlik.
*Badly*, badiko, badliko.
*Bake*, bakön.
*Baker*, bakel.
*Bath*, ban.
*Bathe*, banön.
*Bavaria*, Bayän.
*Bavarian* (noun), Bayänel.
*Be* (verb), binön.
*Beauty*, jön, venud.
*Beautifully*, jönik.
*Because*, bi.
*Become* (verb), vedön.
*Bed*, bed.
*Beer*, bil.
*Befall, overtake, surprise*, süpitön.
*Before* (locally), bif.
*Before* (temporally), büfo.
*Beg* (verb), begön.
*Begin*, beginön.
*Beginning, commencement,* [begin.
*Behold here*, eko.
*Being* (noun), bin.
*Belief*, klöd.
*Believe* (verb), klödön.
*Belgium*, Beljän.
*Belong*, lönön.
*Below*, diso.
*Betroth*, matapömetön.
*Beverage*, dlin.
*Beyond the sea, transoceanic*, lovemelik.
*Big, large, great*, gletik.
*Bill of exchange*, cänapened.
*Bird*, böd.
*Birth*, motöf.
*Black* (adj.), blägik.
*Blackness*, bläg.
*Blessed*, beatik.
*Blow, slap* (noun), flap.
*Book*, buk.

*Boot*, but.
*Booty, prey*, lapin.
*Botany*, planav.
*Bottom, foundation*, stab.
*Both*, bofik.
*Boudoir, small room*, smacem.
*Boy*, pul.
*Branch, twig*, tuig.
*Bravely*, lanimelik.
*Bravo!* bafö!
*Break* (verb), blekön.
*Bread*, bod.
*Breast*, blöt.
*Breath*, bläd.
*Bridge*, pon.
*Bring*, blinön.
*Brother*, blod.
*Build* (verb), bumön.
*Building* (noun), bumot.
*Burn* (verb), filedön.
*But*, ab, yed.
*Butler*, bötel.
*Butter*, mileg.
*Butterfly*, pab.
*Buy*, lemön.
*By, at*, len.
*By means of*, dub.

### C.

*Calculate, reckon*, kalön.
*Calculation, account*, kal.
*Calender, almanac*, kaled.
*Can, be able*, kanön.
*Cannon*, kän.
*Cap*, luhät.
*Capital, chief city*, glezif.
*Cargo, load, freight*, fled, lodam.
*Carry* (verb), polön.
*Carriage, wagon*, vab.
*Cart*, vab.
*Cast, throw* (verb), jedön.
*Cat*, kat.
*Catch sight of*, dalogön.
*Caterpillar*, lupab.
*Cause* (noun), kod.
*Cause* (verb), kodön.
*Cave*, ninavag.
*Celebrated, famous*, mäkabik.

*Century*, yelatum.
*Certainly, indeed*, dido.
*Challenge, summon* (verb), suflagön.
*Chance*, fäd.
*Charm, beauty*, venud.
*Chase, hunt*, yag.
*Cheese*, fomad.
*Chemistry*, kiem.
*Child*, cil.
*Chili*, Cilän.
*China*, Cinän.
*Christ*, Krit.
*Christian* (adj.). kritik.
*Christianity*, kritav.
*Christendom*, kritef.
*Church*, glüg.
*Cigar*, zigad.
*Cigarette*, smazigad.
*Circle*, züm.
*Circular* (noun), zülag.
*City, town*, zif.
*Classification, grouping*, nindilam.
*Classify*, nindilön.
*Clay*, taim.
*Clear, loud*, kleilik, klülik.
*Cloth*, klöf.
*Coast, shore*, jol.
*Coffee*, kaf.
*Cold* (noun), kalod.
*Cold* (adj.), kalodik.
*Combat* (noun), komip.
*Combat* (verb), komipön.
*Combatant*, komipel.
*Come*. kömön.
*Comedy*, yofapled.
*Commencement, begin*.
*Commerce, trade*, ted.
*Common, in common, together*, tugedik.
*Company*, sog.
*Comprehend*, suemön.
*Concerning, of*, dö.
*Concert*, konzed.
*Conflagration*, filed.
*Conquer* (verb), vikodön.
*Consecration festival*, kosek.
*Consent* (noun), zepam.
*Consent* (verb), zepön.

*Consider, regard*, konsidön.
*Consider, meditate, think*, meditön.
*Consideration*, tikam.
*Constancy*, stanöf.
*Constitution, nature of things*, liköf.
*Consume, use up*, fegebön.
*Continent, large mass of land*, fimän.
*Conversation, dialogue*, pükot.
*Cook* (noun), kukel.
*Cook* (verb), kukön.
*Copy-book* (Fr.cahier), pöpem.
*Cordially, heartily*, ladlik.
*Corpse*, fun.
*Cost* (verb), kostön.
*Costly*, delidik.
*Count* (verb), numön.
*Count, earl*, gab.
*Country, land*, län.
*Court of justice, tribunal*, cödef.
*Cousin* (m), kösel.
*Crockery*, domem taimik.
*Cry* (verb), vokön.
*Cunning, sly*, käfik.
*Custom, import or export duty*, tolad.
*Custom-house officer*, toladal.

D.

*Daily, every day*, vadelo.
*Danger*, pölig.
*Dangerous*, pöligik.
*Day*, del.
*Dear*, delidik.
*Dearth*, delid.
*Debt*, deb.
*Dear, beloved*, löfik.
*Death*, deil.
*Deceased*, beatik.
*December*, Balsetelul. [kön.
*Dedicate, devote* (verb), köse-
*Defence, resistance*, tasteifam.
*Delight, merriment*, yof.
*Derivation,* } deköm.
*Descent,*
*Descend, set, go down*, disön.
*Describe*, beponön.

*Desert (at dinner)*, postab, (cf. tab.).
*Design, intention*, desän.
*Designedly*, desäno.
*Destroy, pull down*, distukön.
*Devotion, worship*, devod.
*Devotional*, devotik.
*Die*, deilön.
*Different*, difik.
*Difficult, hard*, fikulik.
*Dine, eat*, fidön.
*Disciple, follower, adherent*, züpel.
*Dialogue, conversation*, pükot.
*Discover* (verb), datuvön.
*Discovery*, datüv.
*Disgrace*, jemod.
*Distance*, fag.
*Distant*, fagik.
*Distinguished*, sikik.
*Disturb* (verb), tupön.
*Do* (verb), dunön.
*Dog*, dog.
*Door*, yan.
*Double* (verb), telön.
*Dowry*, blim.
*Drama*, dam.
*Dread, fear* (noun), dled.
*Dread, fear* (verb). dledön.
*Dwell, inhabit*, lödön.
*Duchy*, dükän, ledükän.
*Duck*, dök.
*Duke*, dük.
*Durability*, dulöf.
*Duration*, dul.
*Duty (on import or export)*, tolad.

E

*Each*, alik.
*Each other*, balvoto.
*Ear*, lil.
*Earthen, made of clay*, taimik.
*Earl, count*, gab.
*Earthenware, domem* taimik.
*East, orient*, lefüd.
*Easy*, nefikulik.
*Echo*, lek.

*Economical, sparing, thrifty*, spälik.
*Economize, save up, put by*, spälön.
*Edifice, structure*, stuk.
*Eat, dine*, fidön.
*Education*, dadnk.
*Eel*, snekafit.
*Egypt*, Ägüpän.
*Egyptian* (noun), Agüpäncl.
*Eight*, jöl.
*Elapse, pass away, perish*, fegolön.
*Empire, kingdom*, kinän.
*Encircle, surround*, zümön.
*End*, fin.
*Endure, last*, dulön.
*Enemy*, neflen.
*Engage, promise*, pömetön.
*England*, Nelijän.
*Englishman*, Nelijel.
*English* (Adj.), Nelijik.
*Enter*, nitlidön.
*Enjoy*, juitön.
*Enlargement, expansion, increase*, gletam.
*Entrust, trust* (verb), konfidön.
*Equipment*, blim.
*Escape, run away* (verb), mogonön.
*Espy*, dalogön.
*Essence*, binug.
*Estate*, gued.
*Eternal*, telnalik.
*Europe*, Yulop.
*European* (noun), Yulopel.
*Evening*, vendel.
*Everywhere, universally*, valiko.
*Ever (at any time)*, evelo.
*Every*, alik.
*Exaggerate* (verb), tudunön.
*Excellent*, bizugik.
*Except*, plä.
*Exercise, task*, sugiv.
*Exclaim* (verb), sevokön.
*Exist* (Fr. se trouver), sibinön, stadön.
*Expansion, increase, enlargement*, gletam.

*Expensive*, delidik.
*Extend, stretch* (verb), setenön.

## F.

*Fall* (verb), falön.
*Fall, slip* (verb), slifön.
*Fall ill* (verb), maládön.
*Fame*, mäkab.
*Famous, celebrated*, mäkabik.
*Far*, fagik.
*Father*, fat.
*Fatherland*, fatän.
*Fear, dread* (noun), dled.
*Fear, dread* (verb), dledön.
*February*, Telul.
*Feel* (verb), senön.
*Feel, perceive* (verb), senitön.
*Fell* (verb), fälön.
*Festive, solemn*, zelik.
*Festive mood*, zeläl.
*Festivity*, zel.
*Few, a few*, anik, nemödik.
*Field, acre*, feil.
*Fill* (verb), fulön.
*Find* (verb), tuvön.
*Finger*, fined.
*Fire*, fil.
*Firmament, sky*, sil.
*First*, balid.
*Firstly*, balido.
*First of exchange*, cünapened balid.
*Fish*, fit.
*Fit, suitable, appropriate*, dleföl.
*Five*, lul.
*Flesh, meat*, mit.
*Flight* (from fly), flit.
*Flight* (from flee), fug.
*Flow* (verb), flumön.
*Flower*, flol.
*Follow* (verb), sukön.
*Follower, adherent, disciple*, zűpel.
*Food, nourishment*, nulűd.
*Food*, zib.
*Foot*, fut.
*Foot, on foot*, futo.
*Footstep*, futaveged.

*For* (prep.), plo.
*Foreigner*, foginel.
*Forest*, fot.
*Forgive, pardon*, fögivön.
*Formerly, once upon a time*, vöno.
*Forthwith, immediately, anon*, foviko.
*Fortune, luck*, läb.
*Fortunate, lucky*, läbik.
*Foundation, bottom*, stab.
*Four*, fol.
*Fox*, foxaf.
*Fracture*, blek.
*France*, Flent, Flentän.
*Free, open*, libik.
*Freeze*, flodön.
*Freight, cargo, load*, lodam.
*French* (adj.), Flentik.
*Frenchman*, Flentel.
*Fresh* (adj.), flifik.
*Freshness*, flif.
*Friday*, Mälüdel.
*Friend*, flen.
*Friendliness*, flenöf.
*Friendship*, flenüg.
*Fright, terror*, tlep.
*Front, in front* (locally), bifo.
*Fruit* (Lat. frux), fluk.
*Fruit* (Lat. promum), pom.
*Further, in future*, fälo.

FROM . Des

## G.

*Garden*, gad.
*Gardener*, gadel.
*Garden tools*, gadem.
*Garment*, klot.
*Gate*, leyan.
*Generally*, valiko.
*Gently, softly*, lovik.
*Geography*, taled.
*Geology*, talav.
*German* (adj.), Deutik.
*German* (noun), Deutel.
*Germany*, Deutän.
*Get* (verb), getön.
*Get up, rise*, sustanön.
*Gift, present*, legivot.
*Give* (verb), givön.

*Gladden*, gälön.
*Glass, tumbler*, glät.
*Gloom*, glum.
*Go*, golön.
*Go down, descend, set*, disön.
*Go by, go past*, beigolön.
*Goal*, zeil.
*God*, god.
*Gold*, golüd.
*Good* (adj.), benik, gudik.
*Good man*, gudikel.
*Goodness*, gud.
*Goods, wares*, can.
*Gracious*, benik.
*Gram*, glam.
*Grandfather*, fatel.
*Grandduke*, ledük.
*Grasp* (verb), dasumön.
*Grateful*, danik.
*Great, large, big*, gletik.
*Greece*, Glik.
*Greek* (noun), Glikel.
*Green*, glün.
*Greens, vegetables*, glüned.
*Growl*, dibatonön.
*Guest*, lot.
*Gun*, gün.
*Gunpowder*, günapur.

## H.

*Habitually*, kösemo.
*Hair*, hel.
*Half*, (noun, Fr. moitié), laf.
*Half-year*, lafayel.
*Hand*, nam.
*Haply, by chance*, fädiko.
*Happy*, beatik.
*Hard, difficult*, fikulik.
*Hardly*, töbo.
*Hare*, liev.
*Hasten*, spidön.
*Haven, port*, pof.
*Hat*, hät.
*Hatred*, het.
*Have*, labön.
*Head*, kap.
*Health*, saun.
*Healthy*, saunik.
*Hear*, lilön.

*Heart*, lad.
*Heartily, cordially*, ladlik.
*Heat*, hit.
*Heavy*, vetik.
*Height, summit*, geil.
*Helmet*, lehüt.
*Help*, yuf.
*Here*, is.
*Hesitate*, süenön.
*Hiding-place, loop-hole, shelter*, slupöp.
*High*, geilik.
*Himself, herself, itself*, okik.
*His, her*, ofik, omik.
*Hit* (the mark, verb), dlcfön.
*Hit, strike*, flapön.
*Hitherto*, jünu.
*Hoary-headed*, bäledanik.
*Honour* (noun), stim.
*Hope* (noun), spel.
*Horse*, jeval
*Horseman, horse-soldier*, jevalel.
*Hostelry* (see hotel).
*Hotel*, lotöp, lotug.
*Hour*, düp.
*House*, dom.
*House-gear*, domem.
*How?* liko?
*However*, ga.
*How much?* limödik?
*Humanity, mankind*, menad.
*Hundred*, tum.
*Hungary*, Nugän
*Hunt, chase*, yag.
*Hunt* (verb), yagön.
*Huntsman*, yagel.
*Hurt*, dam.
*Husband*, matel.
*Hut*, ludom.

## I.

*I*, ob.
*Ice*, glad.
*If*, if.
*Ill*, bad.
*Ill, sick*, malädik.
*Immediately, forthwith, anon*, foviko, lenu.
*Important*, veütik.

*In*, in.
*Increase, expansion, enlargement*, gletam.
*Indeed, certainly*, dido.
*India*, Nidän.
*Indicate, announce*, malön.
*Induce, urge*, stigön.
*Industrious*, dutik.
*Industry*, dut.
*Inhabit, dwell*, lödön.
*Inhabitant*, ninlödel.
*Injury*, däm.
*Injure*, dämön.
*Inn, hotel, hostelry*, lotöp,
*Inside*, ino. [lotug.
*Insure*, sefön.
*Inspect, survey*, sulogön.
*Instruction, lesson, act of teaching*, tid.
*Intelligence*, kapäl, kapälüb.
*Intelligent*, kapälik.
*Intention*, desän.
*Intentionally*, desäno.
*Invent*, datikön.
*Invention*, datuv.
*Investigate*, vestigön.
*Invigorate*, nämön.
*Iron*, lel.
*Italy*, täl, tälän.

J.
*January*, Balul.
*Journey, voyage*, täv.
*Joy*, gäl.
*Judge* (noun), cödel.
*Judge* (verb), cödön.
*Jurisprudence*, gitav.
*July*, Velul.
*June*, Mälul.
*Justice*, cöd.

K.
*Kettle*, caf.
*Kill*, funön.
*Kilogram*, miglam.
*Kilometre*, milmet.
*King*, reg.
*Kingdom, empire*, kinän.
*Kitchen*, kuk.
*Kitchen-knife*, kukaneif.

*Knife*, neif.
*Know* (verb), nolön.
*Know* (Fr. connaître), sevön.
*Knowledge*, nol.

L.
*Lady*, läd.
*Lake*, lak.
*Land, country*, län.
*Landscape, region*, topöf.
*Large, great, big*. gletik.
*Last, endure*, dulön.
*Last* (adj.), lätik.
*Last evening*, ävendelo.
*Last year*, ayelo.
*Late*, lat.
*Latitude, width*, vid.
*Laugh, smile* (verb), smilön.
*Lead* (verb), dugön.
*Learn, become aware of*, plakön.
*Leather*, skit.
*Left, not right*, nedet.
*Lend*, lugivön.
*Length*, loned.
*Lengthen*, lonedön.
*Lesson, act of teaching, instruction*, tid.
*Let*, letön.
*Letter* (Lat. epistola), pened.
*Liberate, set free*, libön.
*Liberty*, lib.
*Life*, life.
*Lifetime*, lifüp.
*Light, not heavy*, leitik.
*Light up* (verb), dalitön.
*Lion*, lein.
*Lip*. lip.
*Listen to*, lenlilön.
*Live* (verb), lifön. [lodam.
*Load, freight, cargo*, fled,
*Load* (verb), lodön, suseitön.
*Logic*, tikav.
*Loop-hole, hiding-place, shelter*,
*Loud, clear*, kleilik. [slupöp.
*Love* (verb), löfön.
*Loved, dear*, löfik.
*Lover*, löfan.
*Luck, fortune*, läb.
*Lucky, fortunate*, läbik.
*Luckily*, läbo.

## M.

*Magnitude*, glet.
*Majesty*, mayed.
*Man* (Lat. vir), man.
*Man* (Lat. homo), men.
*Mankind, humanity*, menad.
*Many*, mödiks.
*Many a one*, teldik.
*March* (the month), kilul.
*Marriage*, mat, mated.
*Master*, masel.
*Master, Mr., Sir*, Söl.
*Material, stuff*, stof.
*Mathematics*, gletav.
*Matrimony*, mat, mated.
*Mature, ripe*, madik.
*Maturity*, mad.
*May* (the month), Lulul.
*Means, by means of*, dub.
*Meat, flesh*, mit.
*Medicine*, medin. [nav.
*Medicine, the science of*, medi-
*Meditate, consider, think*, meditön.
*Melancholy, sadness*, luladel.
*Merchandise*, can.
*Merchant* (wholesale), tedal.
*Merchant* (retail), tedel.
*Merriment, delight*, yof.
*Meter* (39·37 in.), met.
*Midday*, zeudel.
*Middle, in the midst*, zenodü.
*Midnight*, zeneit.
*Might, power*, mekad.
*Mighty, powerful*, mekadik.
*Mile*, leil.
*Milk*, milig.
*Million*, balion.
*Mine (a)*, meinöp.
*Mineral*, min.
*Mineralogy*, minav.
*Mingle, mix*, migön.
*Minister, servant*, dünal.
*Mislead, seduce*, fedugön.
*Miss, young lady*, vomül.
*Mix, mingle*, migön.
*Moderation*, mafof.
*Moisten, wet*, luimön.
*Moment*, timil.
*Momentarily*, timilo.

*Monday*, Telüdel.
*Money*, mon.
*Monkey, ape*, lep.
*Monster*, tuvemaf.
*Month*, mul.
*Mood*, ladälod.
*Moon*, mun.
*Morning*, gödel.
*Mother*, mot.
*Mountain*, bel.
*Mountain-range*, belem.
*Move* (verb), mofön.
*Much*, mödik, mödo.
*Mule*, mucuk.
*Music*, musig.
*Musician*, musigel.
*Must* (verb), mütön.
*Mutually*, balvoto.
*My*, obik.

## N.

*Name* (noun), nem.
*Name* (verb), nemön.
*Narrate*, konön.
*Narrative, story*, kon.
*Native of*, motöfik.
*Native town*, motöfazif.
*Nature*, nat.
*Natural science*, natav.
*Near*, nilik.
*Near by*, neb, nilü.
*Necessary*, zesüdik.
*Need, want* (verb), nedön.
*Needful*, zesüdik.
*Needle*, nad.
*Neighbourhood, vicinity*, nil.
*Neighbour*, nilel.
*Neither...nor*, ni...ni.
*Nephew*, nef.
*Nest*, smabed.
*Never*, negelo, nevelo.
*Nevertheless*, deno.
*New*, nulik.
*Night*, neit.
*No. none*, nonik.
*Nobody*, nek.
*North*, nolüd.
*North America*, Nolü Melop.
*North American* (noun), Nolü Melopel.

*Nose,* nud.
*Not very,* nö.
*Not yet,* no nog.
*Nothing,* nos.
*Nourishment, food,* nulüd.
*November,* Balsebalul.
*Now,* nu.
*Number* (noun), num.
*Number, count* (verb), numön.

## O.

*Oats,* zab.
*Occasionally, at times,* sotimo.
*October,* Balsul.
*Of,* de.
*Of, concerning,* dö.
*Officer,* fizir.
*Often,* ofen.
*On, up, upon,* su.
*One* (numeral), bal.
*Once upon a time, formerly,* vöno.
*Open, free,* libik.
*Opera,* lop.
*Orient, East,* Lefüd.
*Origin,* ved.
*Other,* votik.
*Out, out of,* se.
*Over,* ovi.
*Overtake, surprise,* supitön.

## P.

*Pain,* dol.
*Pair* (noun), telid.
*Palace,* ledom.
*Paper,* pöp.
*Pardon, forgive,* fögivön.
*Parents,* paels.
*Part* (noun), dil.
*Partly,* dilo.
*Pass away, perish, elapse,* fegolön.
*Patient, sufferer,* malüdikel.
*Patriotism,* fatänül.
*Pay* (verb), pelön.
*Pay duty or toll,* toladön.
*Peace,* püd.

*Pear,* bün.
*Peasant,* feilel.
*Pedestrian,* futel.
*Penalty,* pön.
*Pencil,* stib.
*Perceive, feel,* senitön.
*Performance* (on the stage), damatelam.
*Perish, pass away, elapse,* fegolön.
*Permit, allow* (verb), dalön.
*Philology,* pükav.
*Philosophy,* filosop, sapav.
*Physician, surgeon,* medinel, sanel.
*Physics,* füsid.
*Pine-tree,* pein.
*Place* (verb), pladön.
*Plan,* desün.
*Plant,* plan.
*Play, piece* (noun), pled.
*Play* (verb), pledön.
*Please* (verb), plidön.
*Pleasure,* gälod.
*Pluck* (verb), plökön.
*Poem,* poedat.
*Poet,* poedel, poedal.
*Poetry, poesy,* poed.
*Poor,* pöfik.
*Port, haven,* pof.
*Portion,* por.
*Poverty,* pöf.
*Possession,* labed.
*Possible,* mögik.
*Pound, £,* paun.
*Powder,* pur.
*Power, might,* meknd.
*Power, strength, emphasis,* näm.
*Powerful, mighty,* mekadik.
*Praise* (noun), lob.
*Praise* (verb), lobön.
*Prefer,* bizugön.
*Preliminary,* büo.
*Pretend, simulate,* simulön.
*Prey, booty,* lapin.
*Price, sum,* suäm.
*Primarily,* büo.
*Prince,* plin.
*Procure,* lukijafön.
*Professor,* plofed.

*Promise, engage* (verb), pömetön.
*Property, wealth*, labem.
*Prospect, view*, lukilogam.
*Pull down, destroy*, distukön.
*Pupil, scholar*, julel.
*Push* (verb) dlanön.
*Push back*, gedlanön.
*Pyramid*, pir.

## Q.

*Quarter part*, foldil.
*Quick! be quick!* spidö!
*Quintuple*, lulön.

## R.

*Railway*, lelod.
*Rain* (verb), lömibön.
*Read*, liladön.
*Reciprocally*, balvoto.
*Red*, ledik.
*Regard, consider,* konsidön.
*Region, landscape*, topöf.
*Reiterate*, denuön.
*Remain*, blibön.
*Remainder*, lemän.
*Rend*, dimidön.
*Repeat*, denuön.
*Reply* (verb), gesagön.
*Repose* (noun), taked.
*Repose* (verb), takedön.
*Representation* (on the stage), damatelam.
*Request* (noun), beg.
*Request* (verb), begön.
*Resistance, defence*, tasteifam.
*Rest*, tak.
*Restaurant, eating house*, staud.
*Rich, wealthy*, liegik.
*Riches*, lieg.
*Ride* (verb), mönitön.
*Rider* (noun), monitel.
*Right* (Lat. *jus*), git.
*Right hand*, det.
*Right* (not left) detik.
*Ripe, mature*, madik.
*Ripeness, maturity*, mad.
*Rise, get up*, sustanön.
*River*, flum.

*Road, street*, süt.
*Road, way*, veg.
*Roast meat*, loet.
*Rob* (verb), lapinön.
*Robber*, lapinel.
*Roman* (noun), Romel.
*Room* (a), cem.
*Run away, escape*, mogonön.
*Russia*, Lusän.
*Russian* (noun), Lusänel.
*Russian* (adj.), Lusänik.

## S.

*Sack* (noun), sak.
*Sacrifice* (verb), kösefön.
*Sacrifice, devote, dedicate*, (verb), kösekön.
*Sadness, melancholy*, luladül.
*Sage*, sapal.
*Same, the*, ot.
*Save up, put by, economise*, spülön.
*Saxony*, Saxän.
*Say* (verb), sagön.
*Scholar, pupil*, julel.
*Scholar, learned man, savant*, nolel.
*School*, jul.
*Schoolbook*, julabuk.
*Scientific*, nolik.
*Scotland*, Jotän.
*Season*, yelatim.
*Secondly*, telido.
*Secure, safe*, sefik.
*Secure, insure, make safe*, selön.
*Seduce, mislead*, fedugön.
*See* (verb), logön.
*Seek*, sükön.
*Seem, shine, appear*, jinön.
*Seize upon*, dasumön.
*Seldom*, seledik.
*Send away*, desedön.
*September*, Zülul.
*Servant, domestic servant*, dünel.
*Servant, minister*, dünal.
*Serve*, dünön.
*Set, descend, go down*, disön.

*Set, cause to sit*, siadön.
*Seven*, vel.
*Shame*, jem.
*Shameless*, nejemik.
*Shatter, shiver*, diblekön.
*She*, of.
*Shelter, loophole, hiding-place*, slupöp.
*Shine, seem, appear*, jinön.
*Ship*, naf.
*Shiver, shatter*, diblekön.
*Shoe*, juk.
*Shoot*, jutön.
*Shore, coast*, jol.
*Short*, blefik.
*Shrub*, smabim.
*Sick, ill*, maladik.
*Silence*, nepük.
*Silent, to be, keep secret* (verb) (Lat. *silere*), seilön.
*Silent* (adj.), stil.
*Silesia*, Ilesän.
*Simulate, pretend*, simulön.
*Sing*, kanitön.
*Singer, minstrel*, kanitel.
*Single*, dabalik.
*Since*, sis.
*Sir, master, Mr.*, Söl.
*Six*, mäl.
*Skate* (noun), gladajnk.
*Skate* (verb), gladajukön.
*Sky, firmament*, sil.
*Slap, blow* (noun), flap.
*Sleep* (verb), slipön.
*Sleep* (noun), slip.
*Slip* (noun), slup.
*Slip* (verb), slifön, slupön.
*Slip out*, seslupön.
*Sly*, käfik.
*Small*, smalik.
*Smile, laugh* (verb), smilön.
*Smoke* (verb), smokön.
*Snake*, snek.
*Snow* (noun), nif.
*Snow* (verb), nifön.
*So*, so.
*Softly, gently*, lovik.
*Soldier*, solat.
*Solemn, festive*, zelik.
*Some*, anik.

*Some one, a certain one*, sembal.
*Somebody*, ek.
*Son*, son.
*Soon*, suno.
*Soup*, sup.
*Sound loud* (noun), tonod.
*Sorrow*, lüg.
*South*, sulüd.
*Spain*, Spän.
*Sparing, economical, thrifty*, spälik.
*Sparta*, Spartän.
*Spartan* (noun), Spärtanel.
*Speak* (verb), pükön.
*Speak truthfully*, velatön.
*Specially*, pato.
*Speech*, pük, püknd.
*Speed* (noun), spid.
*Spirit*, tikäl.
*Spite, in spite of*, to.
*Sponge*, spog.
*Spread* (verb), pakön.
*Spring* (noun), flolatim.
*Stag*, stäg.
*Stage, theatre*, teat.
*Stand* (noun), stan.
*Start from* (verb), matävön.
*Startled*, pejeköl.
*Starve, suffer want*, dalebön.
*Stay, reside, tarry* (verb), stebön.
*Steam*, stem. [
*Step, stride, wade*, stepön.
*Step, tread* (verb), tlidön.
*Step-father*, lufat.
*Stone* (noun), ston.
*Stop* (verb), stopön.
*Storey, floor* (of a house), stök.
*Story, narrative*, kon.
*Street, road*, süt.
*Stuff, material*, stof.
*Strength, power*, näm.
*Stretch, extend*, setenön.
*Strike, hit* (verb), flapön.
*Stride, step, wade*, stepön.
*Strong, vigorous*, nämik.
*Structure, edifice*, stuk.
*Student*, studel.
*Study* (verb), studön.
*Such*, som.

E

*Suffer* (verb), sufön.
*Suffice, be enough*, sätän.
*Sugar*, jueg.
*Suitable, appropriate, fit*, dleföl.
*Sum, price*, suäm.
*Summer*, hitatim.
*Summit, height*, geil.
*Summon, challenge* (verb),
*Sun*, sol. [suflagön.
*Sunday*, Balüdel.
*Surgeon, physician*, medinel, sanel.
*Surprise, overtake, befall*, süpitön.
*Surround, encircle*, zümön.
*Survey, inspect* (verb), sulogön.
*Swiss* (noun), Iveizel.
*Switzerland*, Iveiz, Iveizän.

### T.

*Table*, tab.
*Take*, sumön.
*Tarry, stay, reside*, stebön.
*Task, exercise*, sugiv.
*Taste* (verb), gutön.
*Tea*, tied.
*Teach* (verb), tidön.
*Teacher*, tidel.
*Tear* (noun), dlen.
*Tear, rend*, dimidön.
*Ten times*, balsna.
*Tenth* (adj.), balsnalik.
*Terminate, flow into* (said of a river), ninflumön.
*Termination, end*, finam.
*Terror, fright*, tlep.
*Than*, ka.
*Thank* (verb), danön.
*Thankful*, danik.
*Thanks!* danü!
*That*, das.
*Theatre, stage*, teat.
*Then*, tän.
*Theologian*, godavel.
*Theology*, godav.
*There*, us.
*Therefore*, sikod.
*Thereto*, alos.

*Theft*, tif.
*Thief*, tif.
*Thing*, din.
*Think* (verb), tikön.
*Think, consider, meditate*, meditön.
*Think of, estimate* (verb), cedön.
*Third* (noun), kilid.
*Thirst*, nelüm.
*This* (person), at.
*This* (thing), atos.
*This* (time), atna.
*Thoroughly, from the bottom*, stabiko.
*Thought* (noun), tik.
*Thousand*, mil.
*Three*, kil.
*Thrifty, economical, sparing*, spälik.
*Through*, da.
*Through, by means of*, dub.
*Throw, cast* (verb), jedön.
*Thuringia*, Türän.
*Thursday*, Lulüdel.
*Thunder* (noun), töt.
*Thunder* (verb), tötön.
*Thy*, olik.
*Ticket*, biliet.
*Till*, jü.
*Time*, tim.
*Trade, commerce*, ted.
*Trade* (verb), tedön.
*Travel* (verb), vegön, tävon
*Travel back*, gevegön.
*Traveller*, tävel.
*Tread, step* (verb), tlidön.
*Treble* (verb), kilön.
*Tree*, bim.
*Treetop*, bimaklon.
*Trifle*, smalöf.
*Trick, stratagem*, küf.
*Tricky, sly*, käfik.
*Triplet*, kilel.
*True*, velatik.
*Truth*, velat.
*To, too*, tu.
*To, towards*, al.
*To-day*, adelo.
*Together, in common, common*, tugedik.

*Together, with,* ko.
*Tobacco,* tabak.
*To-morrow,* odelo.
*Ton* (1,000 kilogs.), toned.
*Tone* (noun), ton.
*Top,* klon.
*Town, city,* zif.
*Tragedy,* lügapled.
*Transoceanic,* lovemelik.
*Trowsers,* blit.
*True, truly,* vo.
*Truly, in faith, in truth,* fe.
*Trust, entrust* (verb), confidön.
*Tuesday,* Kilüdel.
*Tumbler, glass,* glät.
*Turn* (verb), flekön, tulön.
*Twentieth* (adj.), telsnalik.
*Twig, branch,* tuig.
*Two,* tel.

### U.

*Ugly,* hetlik.
*Uncle,* nök.
*Under,* dis.
*Understand* (verb), kapaiön.
*Unfortunately,* liedo.
*Unique,* lebalik.
*University,* niver.
*Universally, everywhere,* valöpo.
*Unless,* nendas.
*Unluckily,* neläbo.
*Up, upon, on,* su.
*Upper,* löpik.
*Upstairs, above,* löpo.
*Urge, induce* (verb), stigön.
*Use* (verb), gebön.
*Use up, consume* (verb), fegebön.

### V.

*Vacuum,* vag.
*Vainly, in vain,* vanlik, vanliko.
*Valley,* nebel.
*Various,* difik.
*Vegetables, greens,* glüned.
*Verse,* liän.
*Very,* vemo.
*Vex* (verb), skanön.
*Vicinity, neighbourhood,* nil.

*Victory,* vikod.
*View, prospect,* lukilogam.
*Vigorous, strong,* nämik.
*Village,* pag.
*Visit* (noun), visit.
*Visit* (verb), visitön.
*Volcano,* filabel.
*Voyage, journey,* täv.

### W.

*Wade, stride, step* (verb), stepön.
*Wagon, cart, carriage,* vab.
*Waistcoat,* blötaklot.
*Wait* (verb), valadön.
*Waiting-room,* valudöp.
*Waiter,* bötel.
*Walk, take a walk* (verb), spatön.
*Walk* (noun), spat.
*Walk, go on foot* (verb), futelön.
*Wall,* völ
*War,* klig.
*Wares,* can.
*Warm,* vamik.
*Warmth,* vam.
*Water,* vat.
*Way, road,* veg.
*Wealth, property,* labem.
*Wealthy, rich,* liegik.
*Weather,* stom.
*Week,* vig.
*Weep* (verb), dlenön.
*Wednesday,* Folüdel.
*Weighty, heavy,* vetik.
*Weighty, important,* veütik.
*Welcome,* vekömo.
*Well* (adv.), beno.
*Well then, also.*
*West,* vesüd.
*Wet, moisten* (verb), luimön.
*When?* kiüp?
*When,* ven.
*Where?* kiöp? kiplad?
*Where* (relat.), kö.
*Wherefore? why?* kikod?
*Which* (person), kel } relat.
*Which* (thing), kelos }

*Whilst*, du.
*Whisper* (verb), lovapükön.
*Whither?* kipladi?
*Whole*, lölik.
*Why? wherefore?* kikod?
*Width, latitude*. vid.
*Will* (verb), vilön.
*Willingly*, viliko.
*Wine*, vin.
*Winter*, nifatim.
*Wipe dry* (verb), neluimön.
*Wisdom*, sap.
*Wish* (verb), vipön.
*With, together with*, ko.
*With, by means of*, me.
*Without* (Lat. sine), nen.
*Without that, unless* (Lat. nisi), nendas.
*Wolf*, ludog.
*Woman*, vom.
*Womanish*, luvomik.
*Womanly*, vomik.
*Wont to be* (verb) (Lat. solere), kösömön..
*Wood*, boad.
*Wooden*, boadik.
*Wool*, lain.
*Word*, röd.

*Work* (noun), vob.
*Work* (verb), vobön.
*Worker, workman*, vobel.
*World*, vol.
*World-speech*, volapük.
*Worship, devotion*, devod.
*Wound* (noun), vun.
*Wound* (verb), vunön.
*Write*, penön.

### X.

### Y.

*Year*, yel.
*Yes*, si.
*Yesterday*, ädelo.
*Young*, yunik.
*Youth* (Lat. juventa), yun.
*Youth, young man*, yunel.
*Youthful*, yunlik.

### Z.

*Zeal*, zil.
*Zealous*, zilik.
*Zoology*, nimav.

www.ingramcontent.com/pod-product-compliance
Lightning Source LLC
Chambersburg PA
CBHW020729100426
42735CB00038B/1314